79

D0855537

Skyline Queen
and the
Merchant Prince

Skyline Queen and the Merchant Prince

THE WOOLWORTH STORY

by
John P. Nichols

TRIDENT PRESS · NEW YORK

To Stella Ann, my wife,
whose confidence I treasure.

Contents

SKYLINE QUEEN

THE MERCHANT PRINCE

Foreword

This is the story of a business, pathfinder in a new mercantile field in the old days, that became perhaps as much a part of the daily lives of generation after generation of people, in general, as the neighborhood motion-picture theater and the home town newspaper, as the old-time iceman and the perennial milkman, because, by multiplying the buy-power of their nickels and dimes, it earned their very large and very steadfast trade.

A man molded that trailblazing business in that new-type retail field that became so familiar an element of the pattern of life of America and, later, of lands beyond the seas. And he himself grew as both grew. This then is also the story of that man who pioneered that field, who conceptualized that business, and who ultimately erected a skyhouse that, in effect, became a living monument of that field, of that business, of that man.

The field was the Five-and-Ten. The business, F. W. Woolworth & Co., first, then F. W. Woolworth Co., today's American Woolworth. The man, Frank Winfield Woolworth, merchant prince. The structure, the lofty Woolworth Building, in New York's historic Lower City, styled "Cathedral of Commerce" by an eminent churchman, dubbed "Queen of the New York Skyline" by an awed New York press when it was so spectacularly dedicated in the earliest days of President Woodrow Wilson's administration.

This author's idea of writing this four-pronged story in just this way has been gestating for some years. It all started when writing the chain store industry's book, *The Chain Store Tells Its Story*. And it matured, in thought and growing interest, some years after he had already written the Woolworth Company's in-depth international history, done for Woolworth, at Woolworth, mainly from Woolworth's own records, for Woolworth's own diverse use, with full benefit of traditional Woolworth courtesy and cooperation.

Initiated by this writer, and product wholly of his pen except when Frank Woolworth's quotations tell his story in his very own words, or where other quotations are elsewhere attributed, this work, *Skyline Queen and the Merchant Prince,* now fulfills the author's long-developing confidence that the integrated story of this field, this business, this man, this edifice, in this related way, deserves sharing with broad audience.

The cast of its characters includes the famed founder-heads of substantial Five-and-Ten companies, each himself a significant contributor to the development of the field of Five-and-Tens, who coordinated his organization within the framework of common purpose in 1912 to form today's F. W. Woolworth Co. In orderly sequence, it includes the successive heads of American Woolworth who, after Frank Woolworth's passing, led Woolworth to its present larger, and still growing, stature as a prime purchasing agent of the consumer.

The author expresses appreciation to Hubert P. Smith, Vice President for Public Affairs, not only for reading the manuscript but also for granting access to such current data as were required to thread the story through Woolworth's 92nd year. For reading the manuscript, he also thanks Olaf H. Hage, the company's Assistant Secretary-Attorney; Arthur M. Gross, its Marketing Director; and John J. McGovern, Editor in Chief of "Woolworth World." And for their interest and courtesy, he extends his thanks to Lester A. Burcham, Chairman of the Board, and to John S. Roberts, President.

Opportunity is grasped here to express gratitude for reading the manuscript to Carl E. Geiger, retired former head of the English Department of The Peddie School, and author of the biography of that school's first century, teacher and friend— and to Capt. John P. Nichols, Jr., who took off-duty time from his work as a B-52 Stratofortress pilot of SAC to read and comment upon his dad's effort to tell, meaningfully, the rich, integrated story of the Five-and-Ten; of Frank Winfield Woolworth, its trailblazer; of the company bearing his name that he shaped, and of the skyscraper honoring his name that he erected.

JOHN P. NICHOLS

CHAPTER I

Midspring Evening 1913

No edifice had ever pierced and lighted New York's skyline above 700 feet, or 50 stories, over sidewalk before that mild, dark spring evening.

Then, in the White House in distant Washington, at exactly 7:30 P.M. that April 24, 1913, President Woodrow Wilson pressed a button.

Suddenly, a brilliantly lighted structural goliath sprang into view in Manhattan's Lower City that dazzled New York and its environs as far as the eye could see. The citizenry was awestruck by the majesty of the scene and by the sheer, light-bathed beauty of the world's tallest skyscraper that so spectacularly made its debut that memorable Thursday evening.

By newsreel, newspaper, magazine and other of that day's media of communication, the word of the new monarch crowning Knickerbocker's skyline was spread around the world.

Standing on land that had been active in the life of New York as far back as its New Amsterdam days—on ground that was only a first-base throw of the spot where General George Washington and his troops had heard the Declaration of

Independence read on July 9, 1776—the building towered a record 792 feet overhead.

Modeled after London's Houses of Parliament, its Gothic beauty on sight inspired the eminent Reverend Dr. S. Parkes Cadman to declare it "Cathedral of Commerce." An enthusiastic press dubbed it "Queen of the New York Skyline." But "Woolworth Building" was then, as now, its name of record.

Fulfilled dream of Frank Winfield Woolworth, the "farm-boy-to-merchant-prince" trailblazer and catalyst of the Five-and-Ten in America and abroad, the Woolworth Building was custom-tailored to his precise specifications at a cold cash cost to him of $13.5 million. On that evening of its formal introduction to the Empire City, it stood tall and admirable as probably the only great building in the country's history to face its dedication without any mortgage whatever and without indebtedness of any kind.

Internal beauty, comfort, safety and convenience, together, had an even greater part in the skyscraper's kaleidoscope of values than its 60-story external elegance.

Its cross-shaped main foyer, with its softly lighted, mosaic-studded dome and marble walls, achieved instant acclamation as a Grand Arcade of truly great distinction.

With a floor area of over 30 acres, the height of each of its floors ranged from a minimum 11 feet to over 20 feet. Had Woolworth wished to restrict each floor to customary 10-foot height, the skyqueen could have had 79 floors instead of 60.

The so-called Cathedral of Commerce, moreover, introduced many "firsts" for the accommodation and safety of F. W. Woolworth Co. and a host of other prestigious tenants.

Its 28 high-speed elevators, each telephone-equipped, not only traveled at a rate of velocity unique in that day but also were air-cushioned for maximum safety. Their floor-to-floor movement was monitored in the Grand Arcade by an electric dispatcher system that was first of its kind in any building.

A rarity in that day, every Woolworth Building stairway was an enclosed fire tower. Among other safeguards, it had special protective devices against lightning. It was the first building to have its own power plant. Besides cleaning, repair and maintenance divisions, it had its own fire, police and detective departments.

Back in the early 1800's, the Hone Mansion, built and occupied by Mayor Philip Hone and his family on the very site of the Woolworth Building, had been a showplace of Old New York. But the Woolworth Building, in its turn, far exceeded its ancestor's attraction as a sightseer's "must." Its renown and curiosity appeal became global. And it earned high honors. Cited, for instance, as the tallest and finest office building in the world, it was awarded the Medal of Honor of Liberal Arts at the Panama-Pacific International Exposition held in San Francisco in 1915.

Back of the Woolworth Building story lies the history of a plot of Manhattan ground, of a man pursuing a vision, and of the international enterprise, uniquely serving the public interest, that he built from scratch, thus enabling him to buy the plot and build the building.

Here's how and why it all started and happened.

CHAPTER II

Before Woolworth

A quarter-century or so after Peter Minuit, Director-General of New Netherland, made that storied deal with the Indians, buying Manhattan Island for trinkets worth about $24, New Amsterdam was a thriving little community of less than a thousand people.

Incorporated as a city on February 2, 1653, New Amsterdam's northern extremity was the fortified wall that stood on what is today's Wall Street. And north of that palisade lay the Flat, or De Vlakte, site of this day's City Hall Park, then a rich pasture for New Amsterdam cattle.

Separated from the Flat, or De Vlakte, by a road that is ancestor of Broad Way, today's Broadway, was the so-called Company Farm. On part of that rich land, but a nod from the windmill that was the skyscraper of that Dutch day, the Woolworth Building was erected nearly three centuries later.

Woolworth Site in New Amsterdam Days

By 1664, Manhattan's days under the Dutch West India Company and the illustrious Peter Stuyvesant were numbered.

Granted all Dutch lands in America in March 1664 by his brother, King Charles II of England, James, Duke of York, promptly dispatched a force that captured New Amsterdam and renamed it New York. Peace then reigned for some nine years.

In August of the ninth year, however, a Dutch naval fleet, with repossession of the city as its mission, plied through the Narrows to New York's Upper Bay and landed troops. Preparatory to siege of New York's fortifications, they bivouacked in the Fields, directly opposite today's Woolworth Building site. The parleys between the invaders and the defenders occurred near, perhaps even on, the skyscraper's ground.

The parleys failed. The Dutch struck. New York fell on August 9, 1673, and became New Orange. Some fifteen months later, though, Holland ceded the city to the English by treaty, and it again became New York.

The Woolworth site was affected by these changes of sovereignty. It became Duke's Farm instead of Company Farm after the English conquest of 1664. It was renamed King's Farm under James II, then Queen's Farm under Anne, Queen of England. It finally became Church Farm after the Crown first leased it, then granted it outright, to Trinity Church about 1705.

Neighbor of New York's New Common

During the early third of the eighteenth century, New York's growth and the leasing of Bowling Green by business forced the populace to turn northward for its meetings, and for its sports and merrymaking on Knickerbocker holidays. Consequently, about 1732, the ground that successively had been known as the Flat, or De Vlakte, under the Dutch, and the Fields under the British, became the Common.

Inns and taverns, quick to follow the crowds, soon abounded along the Common. And among the most popular was Drover's Inn, standing near, perhaps smack on, the ground of the Woolworth Building.

For nearly a third of a century the Common continued serenely as a resort for New York's relaxation. That changed in 1765 with Parliament's enactment of a Stamp Act taxing American colonies. The law became instant cause for violent effect. The Common, locale of festivals and jollification before the tax statute, became the scene thereafter of civil aggression against the Stamp Act specifically, and "taxation without representation" generally.

The despised Stamp Act was eventually repealed. New York, however, still had grievance. Like many of its sibling colonies, it bitterly resented Parliament's increasingly oppressive colonial policy. So-called "Liberty Poles" flourished on the Common symbolizing civil resistance. Skirmishes between "redcoats" and "patriots" became commonplace on the Common.

Revolutionary war capped the climax. On July 9, 1776, General George Washington and his troops heard the Declaration of Independence read on the Common, only a sprint distance from the Woolworth site. That September, New York fell to the British.

Hone Mansion as Knickerbocker Showplace

After America won its independence and New York was evacuated in 1783, great change occurred in the Empire City. A grid of financial and business establishments sank deep roots in what is today's Wall Street. Prodded by the encroachment, the city's smart residential district headed northward toward the Common. Part of the Common became a park.

The construction of today's City Hall was commenced in 1803 on part of that park. The completed edifice was dedicated in May 1812.

Elegant homes began to line Broad Way, the city's most fashionable new avenue. One of these, the famed Hone Mansion, stood on the very ground on which the Woolworth Building rose years later. So sumptuous was it, within the limitations of that day, that it became a pride of Old New York.

Like Frank Woolworth, the land's later owner, Philip Hone was a master merchant and a patron of the arts. He was also Mayor of the city during the 1826–1827 period, the city's 57th Mayor.

The Hones entertained frequently and with distinction in their imposing Broad Way home. Prominent figures in national and city affairs were friends and guests. Washington Irving, James Fenimore Cooper, Samuel Woodworth, Fitz-Greene Halleck, John Rodman Drake and other distinguished American authors were often entertained at Hone Mansion.

These were glory days for Broad Way, the smart residential avenue that, in a prior day, had been the path that Boston post riders used on courier service between infant New York and infant Boston. But its days of glory were numbered. It fell as an elite residential street before the relentless expansion of business and its grabs of the tree-lined residential streets and lanes of Old New York.

Site Fades as Carriage Trade Retreats

Mansions and commodious residences beat a hasty retreat northward as the thrust of business invasion accelerated. Moving uptown in 1836, the Philip Hones were among the earliest to depart the Lower City. The lower floors of the Hone

Mansion were then converted into stores. The American Hotel, next door, annexed the upper floors.

Within two decades, Broad Way, now Broadway, was a busy street heavy with the traffic of horse-drawn business vehicles. Platoon after platoon of business buildings of nearly equal height were aligned along it like a battalion on review.

In 1854, five business buildings, each of five stories, occupied the Broadway site between Barclay Street and Park Place, locale of today's Woolworth Building. The Broadway Bank had the corner location. The four other occupants of that block were a daguerreotype depot, a hair-dye establishment, an umbrella-and-parasol warehouse, and a clothing house. The famed Astor House was located in the very next block.

Neighbor of the Woolworth Building site since 1754, Kings College, that had become Columbia College in 1784, still occupied its Park Place property in 1854. It followed the uptown migration in 1857, however, by moving to its new East 49th Street campus, then later to Morningside Heights.

Woolworth Taps Site for New Glory

Business had not only subjugated most of the historic sections of the Lower City by 1889 but also had made incredible progress in its uptown invasion of Manhattan, a fast-expanding community.

Business gained elbow room, moreover, by reaching skyward besides striking northward. Influenced by the erection in 1884 of the 11-story Home Insurance Building in Chicago, first building to use iron as a structural skeleton, New York's Tower Building was built at 50 Broadway in 1889 to a height of some dozen stories. It was Manhattan's first structural titan.

Where the low brick dwellings of the founding fathers of

New Amsterdam had stood, gable end toward street, in the Lower City's infancy, ever taller business buildings proliferated as the Empire City passed into the twentieth century.

Within still another decade, Manhattan's tall buildings were dwarfed by even taller giants. Scaling 612 feet and 47 stories over 149 Broadway stood the Singer Building, then the Lower City's highest edifice. But only a few miles north of it was the high and mighty Metropolitan Life Building, the era's behemoth. Its 700-foot skyheight made that Madison Avenue goliath the world's tallest office structure. It was exceeded in height only by the Eiffel Tower in Paris, not a building.

But no notable structure, big or little, then occupied the soil of today's Woolworth Building. Oppressed by five dilapidated business buildings, the block fronting Broadway between Barclay Street and Park Place was tired, shabby and frustrated in 1909, a far cry from its Old New York opulence. But it was being observed and appraised.

In the Stewart Building just across City Hall Park, F. W. Woolworth was preparing to harness still another dream. And in its fruition, the historic choice plot that he had been evaluating would not only be rehabilitated but would also gain renown unparalleled in its 300-year history.

On that ground would stand the living monument of the mercantile institution multiplying the buying power of the nickels and dimes of American consumers that he built from scratch as follows.

CHAPTER III

Five-and-Ten

Frank Winfield Woolworth, elder son of farmer John Hubbell and Fanny (McBrier) Woolworth, was born in Rodman, Jefferson County, New York, on April 13, 1852. He spent his boyhood and earliest young manhood, however, on the 108-acre farm just outside the tiny village of Great Bend, New York, to which his father moved his family when Frank was seven and his brother, Charles Sumner, was three.

Frank and Sum (as Charles Sumner was called) were educated in the local common school. They also worked long and hard at their father's side as he battled to make ends meet in those hard times that bridged the Panic of 1857 and the Civil War and its aftermath.

To emancipate himself from farming and to work in a store, perhaps one day to own one, was Frank's two-pronged boyhood dream. Often of an evening, after the long farm day had ended, he and Sum would arrange a make-believe stock of merchandise on the dining room table and sell goods to imaginary customers.

"Too young, too green" were merchants' answers as tall, blue-eyed Frank combed the area for a store post after completing a brief course in a Watertown, New York, commercial college. But in mid-March 1873, on the eve of his twenty-first birthday, he finally landed the full-time store job that patterned his career. He was hired, on a three-months' trial basis without pay, as a combination stockroom boy, errand boy, general handyman, and relief clerk, by the Corner Store of Augsbury & Moore, a leading dry goods store and wholesale house on Watertown's public square. He was hired by William Harvey Moore himself. A relationship was started that forenoon that, in deep friendship, respect and mutual assistance, was to span four decades.

A short time after that hiring, Augsbury & Moore became Moore & Smith, the emporium in which not only Frank Woolworth but also Charles Sumner Woolworth and Fred Morgan Kirby apprenticed in retailing. It was training ground, too, of Carson C. Peck, Clinton Pierce Case, Harry A. Moody —each, later, a master merchant closely associated with the elder Woolworth. And the dynamic Mrs. A. C. Coons, senior clerk under whose eye Woolworth worked when hired, was also to become an important early Woolworth syndicate associate. Known and respected throughout his syndicate as the "Lady of Syracuse," she managed his first Syracuse store with an iron hand and wide appeal—Woolworth's first woman store manager. But that's all ahead.

Counter That Glorified Nickels

This was the golden era of the sellers' market, the power day of the middleman. *Caveat emptor* reigned.

Manufacturers were intent wholly upon turning out goods. Once the goods were fabricated, the producer relied entirely upon the middleman and his drummers for distribution. Lacking direct contact with producers, merchants had no alternative than to depend upon those middlemen for supply. They had no choice than to pay the least high price that intrepid haggling could attain for them. If the consumer had a voice at all during these days of resultant sky-high retail prices, it was wan and weak and unheard.

For the consumer, moreover, this was a day of concealed merchandise. In the usual emporium, customers were expected to make their wants known to the clerk forthwith. Then and then only, generally, were the sought goods taken from inaccessible shelves or from under counters.

These were the days, furthermore, when merchants usually marked the sales price as well as the cost price on the sales ticket, usually in code. Actually, two selling prices were generally indicated, namely an asking price that the storekeeper first tried to get, then a lower price that he would dramatically accept if the customer seriously resisted the first quotation. *Caveat emptor!* "Let the buyer beware!"

Frank Woolworth began his mercantile career at the Corner Store against this background. Five years later, now married to Jennie Creighton, a twenty-three-year-old seamstress from Picton, Ontario, Canada, he was Chief Clerk of Moore & Smith, and was earning the then princely wage of $10 a week. But Moore & Smith was in deep financial trouble.

By 1878, a widespread period of acute business depression, the big New York and Boston jobbing houses had flooded that so-called North Country with zealous and persuasive drummers who had succeeded in seriously overstocking the merchants of that area. Moore & Smith, for instance, found itself with a then massive $35,000 worth of surplus dry goods, notions and jewelry on hand that had to be negotiated into cash forthwith so as to meet payroll and other pressing obligations. Traffic was becalmed. Trade, hence, was motionless. Moore & Smith needed a miracle. It had to contrive a sales stimulus that would, at once, profitably dispose its surplus stock.

From a drummer, William Moore and his partner, Perry Smith, had heard of an "Any Article on This Counter, 5¢" experiment that had recently been made in a Michigan town, probably Port Huron. Reportedly, customers had hungrily gobbled up all of the articles on that counter. And while in the store, they had also bought up an unexpected abundance of higher-priced merchandise. Reluctantly, Moore and Smith decided to try the experiment too.

Choosing to introduce the Moore & Smith counter on the opening day of Watertown's County Fair ". . . when our competitors would be too busy to laugh at us if we fail," Moore rushed a $100 order to Spellman Brothers, New York, for a supply of tin pans, washbasins, buttonhooks, dippers, turkey-red napkins and other so-called "Yankee Notions" to sell for 5¢ apiece.[1]

Frank Woolworth improvised a counter and positioned it in the most conspicuous point in the Corner Store. On it he featured Spellman's "Yankee Notions." He sweetened them with much Moore & Smith surplus stock—"stickers" and "chestnuts," in his parlance, that for months had failed to sell. Over the display, he nailed a homemade sign, "Any Article on This Counter, 5¢."

What a day for Moore & Smith, and for Frank Woolworth, was that Watertown County Fair opening day! "Immediately, things began to happen," Woolworth recounted years later. "Like magic, the goods on the '5¢ counter' faded away and money flowed into the cash drawer."

More and more of Moore & Smith "chestnuts" were piled

---

[1] Silver coins had practically disappeared during the Civil War. The Government, as stopgap, issued fractional currency or so-called "shin plasters" in denominations of 3¢, 5¢, 10¢, 15¢, 25¢ and 50¢. In 1875, Congress enacted a law providing for the replacement of fractional currency by silver coins "as rapidly as possible," and for the redemption of "shin plasters," on demand, in hard money after January 1, 1879. So, this counter's sales were for "shin plasters," as were Woolworth's sales, to about 1880.

on that hungry counter. The throngs scrapped for the bargains. While in the store, they also snapped up other surplus goods at higher prices. By its sensational performance that opening day, and continuance for some days thereafter, the "5¢ counter" turned out to be the bonanza so sorely needed by William Moore and Perry Smith. And the experience was a turning point in the life and career of F. W. Woolworth.

The experiment's success made a deep impression on young Woolworth, veritably shook him up. The more he pondered, the more convinced he became that an effectively operated store stocked exclusively with fast-turning 5¢ goods could prove lastingly successful.

Early in February 1879, with assured credit at Moore & Smith for $315.41 worth of "Yankee Notions," and with William Moore's blessings, Frank Woolworth set forth to blaze the trail of the durable store that, in a period of rampant *caveat emptor,* would bring merchandise values to consumers in wide-open display, at one clearly identified fixed low price.

Emporium That Launched Woolworth

Woolworth's first "Great 5¢ Store" opened in Utica, New York, on February 22, 1879—Washington's birthday, but not yet a legal holiday in New York State. Handbills listing the goods to be offered by the tiny shop off Utica's beaten track had been widely distributed in the 35,000-person municipality by the dynamic twenty-seven-year-old proprietor.

On the eve of that opening occurred the incident that Woolworth was to remember with sentiment mixed with disappointment for the rest of his life.

At about 6 P.M. that Friday evening, a knock was heard at the door of the store as it neared readiness for debut on the morrow. Woolworth himself answered. A woman faced him.

"I'd like to buy a fire shovel," she said, pointing to his circular in her hand that listed fire shovels at 5¢ each.

"Very well, madam," replied Woolworth. "Just step inside and I'll wrap it up for you." She did so and he sold her the shovel.

It is impossible even to estimate the billions of men, women and children of all classes, creeds, colors and nationalities to whom Woolworth stores have sold, here and around the world, in the 93-year lifetime of the Woolworth Company. That lady of Utica, however, was the first. Some forty years after the incident, Frank Woolworth wrote, "She was my first customer, and had I dreamed of the things that were destined to happen to me in subsequent years, I most certainly would have taken her name and kept that money. As it is, I don't even know who she was."

Though the "Great 5¢ Store" drew a crowd on its opening day, it didn't continue to attract steady traffic. In its first week, the tiny pioneering store's sales totaled $244.44, and it maintained about that volume while its novelty lasted. As its novelty faded, however, so too did its sales.

Situated on a side street off the beat of shoppers, the 14-by-25-foot "Great 5¢ Store" did not conveniently bring attractive merchandise to steady traffic but instead depended for life upon enticing shoppers to find its doors. Hence, the handicap of location was emasculating the tiny shop that so vitally needed fast turnover of fixed, low-price merchandise for profitable operation.

By May 1879, Woolworth had net capital of $252.44. His debt to Moore & Smith had been paid. Thus far, he had made money in Utica. He had the confidence of William Moore and the prospect of additional credit. His faith in the "5¢ store" remained unshaken. Weighing these, he made up his mind to close at Utica and to reopen in a robust location commanding steadily heavy traffic.

At 170 North Queen Street, Lancaster, Pennsylvania, then a municipality of 35,000 people, he found and leased his location. For 93 years since then, the name "Woolworth" has been as synonymous with that street as London's stone lions with Piccadilly Circus.

Located on the ground floor of a four-story corner building in the very path of shoppers, the 14-by-35-foot store, at $30-a-month rental, had three show windows to draw customer attention. Here it wouldn't be a case of people finding Woolworth. This time Woolworth was bringing his store to people.

World's Oldest Five-and-Ten

On Saturday, June 21, 1879, F. W. Woolworth's "Great 5¢ Store," mother store of his later network, opened for business in that Lancaster location with a stock of "Yankee Notions" valued at $410, and with seven clerks. By closing time, the browsing crowd had snapped up 31 percent of that stock. Within 26 days, Woolworth had three complete turnovers. Brisk trade became brisker. Each passing day made it clearer to him that he had to open additional stores as promptly as possible.

He recognized that, for mere survival, he had to keep his Lancaster store well stocked with 5¢ goods by tireless safaris in the New York and Philadelphia marketplaces. To go beyond this, to gain optimum progress by profitably bringing higher-priced wants and needs to consumers at fixed nickel prices, he foresaw that, with volume buying, he had to persuade manufacturers to bypass the middleman and sell to him direct, in quantity, for cash, at resultant lower price.

But before he could engage in large-volume buying, he also knew that he had first to achieve large purchasing power, meaning the muscle of large-volume sales. This, then, became his heading, his immediate goal ahead.

He failed in his first two attempts to launch a second durable store. Momentarily impeded in his move for expansion, and otherwise lacking the buying strength to ferret out the wider variety, the more appealing values, needed for his customers at nickel prices, he exercised his only option that summer of 1880. He increased his Lancaster "mother" store's fixed price limit to 10¢, thus making it a Five-and-Ten, world's oldest.[2]

"As soon as we added 10¢ goods to the line," he wrote years later, "we took away part of the '5¢ store's charm'—the charm of finding only one price on a counter, and only one price in a store. But as long as we kept the 5¢ goods on one side of the store and the 10¢ goods on the other, the 'charm' was not entirely lost. It remained a 'charm' just the same." During his lifetime, Woolworth was to rate this 1880 decision at Lancaster as one of the great turning points of his career.

Innovator Builds for Buying Power

To team with his vigorous Lancaster "mother" store, Woolworth opened his second durably successful Five-and-Ten in Reading, Pennsylvania, in September 1884. Then, within the next four trailblazing years, increasingly large, uniformly "redfront" Woolworth units sank deep roots in Harrisburg, Penn-

---

[2] That Corner Store, Watertown, 5¢ counter inspired others besides Frank Woolworth to launch 5¢ stores. In fact, Moore & Smith became the North Country's ace wholesale center for 5¢ goods. But, wrote Woolworth in 1910, "There was not a single 5¢ store in the U.S.A. after 1883 with the exception of Bailey & Co. Like the rest, Bailey drifted into higher and higher prices and perished in the end."

sylvania, Trenton, New Jersey, Elmira, New York, Easton, Pennsylvania, Utica, New York, Wilmington, Delaware, and Allentown, Pennsylvania.

The eight were opened by Woolworth with carefully selected, so-called "partner-managers"—merchants like Carson Peck, Clinton Case and others who later rose to high Woolworth syndicate office. In each case, Woolworth's financial investment in the store was equally matched by his partner. Profits were share and share alike. Woolworth, catalyst, shepherded the network, combed the markets, meshed the links of a growing syndicate bent on maximizing values offered to customers by attaining vast sales volume to achieve vast purchasing power. Each partner, under Woolworth supervision, managed the store in which he himself had financial interest.

Meantime, in 1886, Woolworth had taken his first really great step to make his presence felt in the New York, Boston, Philadelphia, and other Eastern marketplaces of supply. He had moved his family from Lancaster to Brooklyn, and had opened his first New York office at 104 Chambers Street. And on the door of that humble first Woolworth headquarters had appeared, for the first time, the famed Diamond W trademark by which F. W. Woolworth stores were identified from 1886 to 1968. In 1888, he moved his Executive Office to the Stewart Building at 280 Broadway, where, in ever larger and more elegant quarters, it remained until its 1913 ensconcement in Woolworth's own Cathedral of Commerce.

Woolworth was all things to his growing syndicate at this stage. Unassisted, he served as administrator, coordinator, central buyer, bookkeeper, correspondent, inspector, location scout—the gamut—an exacting teacher, an innovator, a self-made master of multi-unit merchandising. In August 1888, he hired Alvin Edgar Ivie, sixteen, as office assistant at $6 per week.

As he smoked out merchandise values for cooperative buying, he specified the available "buys" to his managers through the so-called "Woolworth Approved List" that, at this juncture, was disseminated among them in longhand, on tissue paper. He then pooled store orders and placed them in quantity, for cash, at consequent lower price. Woolworth stores were thus able to sell these "plums" and "corkers" at nickel-and-dime prices, with fair profit.

In addition to laying the foundation of his own syndicate, Woolworth, in this period, also inspired and helped relatives and close friends to enter the field and to grow in it.

He opened a successful store in Scranton, Pennsylvania, in November 1880, for example, with his brother, Sum, as paid store manager. He helped Sum first to buy a half-interest in that store in 1881, then to buy it all in 1883. That unit then became the "mother" store of C. S. Woolworth's own later syndicate. And Sum, in turn, assisted his best friend, Fred Morgan Kirby, to enter the business. Together they opened a profitable emporium in Wilkes-Barre, Pennsylvania, in 1884. Sum then sold Kirby his share in 1887, and that unit became the starting store of F. M. Kirby & Co.

F. W. Woolworth launched a successful store in Erie, Pennsylvania, with his first cousin, Seymour Horace Knox, in 1886; another with Knox in Buffalo in 1888; and with Knox and Edwin Merton McBrier, another cousin, in Lockport, New York, in 1887. Essentially as an accommodation, Woolworth then sold his interest in all three units to Knox in 1889, and they served as the nucleus of S. H. Knox & Co., the large chain subsequently built by Woolworth's favorite cousin.

By 1888–1889, Frank Woolworth's growing fortune enabled him to halt opening new Woolworth stores with "partner-managers." From that juncture forward, he was sole owner of Five-and-Tens added to his network. Streamlined Woolworth stores were opened in Poughkeepsie, New York, Syracuse,

New York and New Haven, Connecticut, on that basis during that two-year period.

With rare flair for managerial selection, he found, trained and assigned effective managers to new units of his growing syndicate. They were employed by Woolworth on the basis of participation in the net profits of the stores that they respectively managed for him, but they themselves made no capital investment whatever. Their annual income depended wholly upon their skill in management, and upon the consequent profitability of their respective stores.

Hence, by year-end 1889, Frank Woolworth had twelve thriving stores in operation. Interestingly, two of those units were managed for him by women. Mary Ann Creighton, his able sister-in-law, managed Poughkeepsie. Mrs. A. C. Coons, indefatigable "Lady of Syracuse," operated that booming Syracuse "red-front."

During that decade of rugged pioneering, Frank Woolworth escalated his sales volume from $12,024 for 1879 to $246,782 for 1889, a minuscule amount by today's standards, yet significant sales might in that era.

But Moore & Smith, as a retail and wholesale house, perished during the decade. Victim of the breakdown of the "5¢ store" boom that had buttressed its wholesale operations, and of the paralyzing of its retail business by the 1883 economic depression, the company was forced to close its doors in 1885.

A friend in need to Frank Woolworth in 1879, William Moore got reciprocation when most needed. With Frank Woolworth's substantial help, the W. H. Moore 5¢ & 10¢ Store had a gala debut later in 1885, located on Moore's famed plot dominating the western extremity of Watertown's public square. So, the former Corner Store flourished as a Five-and-Ten in 1889 on the very ground that the "5¢ counter" had started it all for Woolworth in 1878.

Woolworth Finalizes His Master Plan

Late in 1888, Frank Woolworth was felled by typhoid fever. He was bedridden for nine weeks. As he restlessly recuperated while operating Woolworth practically from his bedstead, he recognized his need for a second in command, and he also finalized the following master plan for developing his syndicate in the immediate future, subject to improvisation as necessary.

1. He pinned down on his map 35 cities east of the Rockies with populations of over 50,000, plus a large number of municipalities with 20,000–50,000 populations, that were prime prospective locales for Woolworth Five-and-Tens.

2. He would train and dispatch one or two men to scout, select, rent, equip and ready stores for opening in those pinpointed communities at the rate of 10–12 per year.

3. He would have another trained specialist who would follow into each such store to lay out the stock, prepare displays, hire help, open the store, then turn it over to its assigned manager for management thereafter.

4. He would select and upgrade a gifted store manager to serve as store inspector on his staff. As such, the inspector would visit all stores periodically and not only check efficiency but also consult with them as to possible improvements in display, ordering, store appearance—the gamut.

5. He would select and promote a highly qualified store manager to the office of General Manager who, under his eye, would relieve him of administrative detail in financial management, personnel administration, and other operating functions.

6. He would select a top-qualified central buyer from among his store managers and assign him to the New York Office. He would choose and add other such volume purchasers as company growth warranted.

7. He would continue to have all purchased goods shipped direct to stores for the present but would open a warehouse, when possible, so as to stock small goods bought in large quantity, for store order, as wanted, at resultant lower price.

Woolworth acted quickly on his master plan after recuperation. "As soon as a business grows beyond one's ability to attend to all of the details himself," he wrote in his daily General Letter, "he must trust to organization and cooperation to carry it forward." He then tapped as his General Manager his Utica, New York "partner-manager," Carson C. Peck.

Starting in the New York Office on January 1, 1890, Peck was not only to become a master merchant, able administrator, and effective developer of manpower but also was to rise later to the very pinnacle of Woolworth leadership as F. W. Woolworth's second in command.

Founder Imprints Indelible Policies

Without even being aware of it, Frank Woolworth, on the basis of performance, was probably one of business history's most effective, instinctive public relations practitioners. He was an intuitive master in establishing and cementing enduring good relations with consumers, communities, suppliers, landlords, employees, banks, government, trade and other of his company's interfacing "publics." He was a catalyst in stimulating cooperative effort towards a common, mutually significant objective. He was an arresting and persuasive communicator despite his limited formal education.

In the vaults of today's F. W. Woolworth Co. in the Woolworth Building, New York, there exist some 187 bound volumes, each large and very thick, containing the General Letters of Frank Woolworth to his store managers from about 1886 through about 1918. On practically a day-to-day basis, those communications detail the intimate, in-depth history of the Five-and-Ten composed by F. W. Woolworth himself, bellwether who stimulated it. Yet he neither intended nor thought of those letters per se as components of historical record.

In the beginning, the daily General Letter, in Woolworth longhand on tissue paper, not only contained the "Woolworth Approved List" identifying available stock for store-manager order but also instructions, announcements, syndicate news, and especially store-management orientation and merchandising counsel.

As the chain grew, the General Letter, now processed, no longer included the Approved List, now separately published. Each letter was now a potpourri of news, announcements, instructions, counsel, anecdotes, the full range of indoctrinational and inspirational material that Woolworth believed significant in welding a burgeoning organization within the framework of common purpose.

Aside from the General Letter, store managers were oriented and developed by the frequent visits of the Chief, and by store-manager conventions that, in effect, were that day's management seminars and workshops. The first was held at the old Hathaway Inn, Darlington, New Jersey, July 17 to 20, 1894.

Inflexible Woolworth policy, monitored and policed by him, was, then, as now, that store managers spend most of their time on the sales floor studying the wants of their own customers, thus enabling each to order his particular store's particular merchandise needs from the Approved List. Relentlessly emphasized, Woolworth, in one General Letter, said:

> Each manager must study the wants of his customers all the time, not try to please his own taste. . . . To illustrate: In years gone by, there used to be demand for certain vases, the ugliest ever made, and I was obliged to buy them against my own taste and judgment. And how they did sell! The same thing applies today. Tastes differ and we must have goods for all.

Woolworth's store managers also had the responsibility of training picked young men, so-called Learners, for upgrading, on merit, to store management from stockroom as the chain gained stature. And managers, of course, had ground-floor opportunity to make headway themselves. Many earned promotion to larger, higher-volume units. Others climbed even higher up the Woolworth ladder.

In 1892, Woolworth buttressed General Manager Peck in the New York Office with Hubert Templeton Parson, first career financial man in the organization. And in 1893, Clinton Pierce Case was promoted from store manager to headquarters, and became the first Woolworth buyer other than the Chief himself to purchase for the Diamond W in foreign markets. Others were upgraded as the company grew.

Though given wide latitude in store operation, in personnel selection and administration, in volume buying from the Approved List, and in other functions of management, each store manager was nevertheless required by contract to conform with the company's Rules & Regulations first formalized by Woolworth in 1892.

Good appearance and considerate, businesslike conduct were exacting Woolworth requirements. A manager was never to be seen coatless on the sales floor, never with his hat on, never to smoke in the presence of customers. He was prohibited from gambling or speculating. He was not permitted to accept any present or gratuity from any source of supply, or from anyone else doing business with Woolworth.

So as to enable each manager to donate to worthy local charities and local welfare enterprises, Woolworth authorized him to expend, at his own discretion, for such purpose, a specified percentage of his previous year's aggregate sales.

Until 1898, each "red-front" was regularly inspected by Woolworth himself. Known as "official visits," his inspections were unannounced, penetrating, painstaking. As visualized in his 1888 master plan, his first store inspector, Charles C. Griswold, was appointed from store ranks in 1898, when the chain's swelling size and the vast demands upon his own time no longer permitted Woolworth to inspect personally. The number of inspectors grew, moreover, as "red-fronts" increased in number. Stores, nevertheless, continued to receive Woolworth visits when least expected.

Woolworth received and studied each inspector's report. Without divulging store identity, he then spread deserving ones into the General Letter, together with his "pro" and "con" comments, for the benefit of all store managers.

Immediately after the calendar year ended, every store manager was required to submit a store inventory to the New York Office reckoning his fiscal year's stewardship.

Woolworth then closeted himself with his aides and audited each such store inventory. Thereafter, the check covering each manager's share of his store's profits was sent to him accompanied by a personal letter from Woolworth evaluating, in detail, his year's store performance.

So as to indoctrinate as well as to stimulate pride of "belonging," Woolworth next prepared his annual letter, and in it he analyzed virtually every facet of Woolworth operation and accomplishment during the ended calendar year.

Managerial "kicks" were favorably regarded and encouraged by Woolworth. "I say 'kick,' " wrote Peck to managers in the Chief's behalf. " 'Kick' on every occasion that warrants it. 'Kick' intelligently so that your 'kick' touches the right spot. If you don't like the goods we buy for you, 'kick.' . . . 'Kick' so that we'll understand your feelings. Don't be satisfied with a simple 'kick,' but explain why you 'kick.' We may 'kick' back, but you're used to that."

World's Products for Main Street

Population grew from about 50 million in 1880 to nearly 63 million in 1890. Manufacturers increased in number during that decade. Value of products fabricated by American factories, and by hand and neighborhood industries, rose from about $5 billion in 1879 to about $9 billion in 1889. The United States ranked first as an industrial nation by 1894 compared with its fourth-place standing in 1860. Wholesale prices were steadily declining. The long-time sellers' market was ebbing. A buyers' market was turning the corner.

The middleman was still the manufacturer's prime reliance for marketing his output as 1890 started. Operating a dozen vigorous "red-fronts" as that year commenced, Woolworth was stocking them through jobbers, certain importers, and by a starting trickle of farsighted producers.

"You are profiting today," recounted Carson Peck to Woolworth men some years later, "from the dreams of a man who was considered a little bit 'wild' only a few years ago—a man who persisted in carrying out his ideas to the letter—who profited by following up his convictions with hard work—and who was happy in being backed up by those in whom he had confidence, and whom he had chosen to assist him."

Peck was very largely referring to the 1890–1900 decade. For Woolworth, always aware of the economic forces at work, that decade was substantially a period of developing organizational sinew, of forging innovative marketing policies, of testing and harnessing merchandising systems and procedures, of steady though conservative growth in number of stores, and of swelling sales volume and purchasing power.

It was a period of continued reinvestment of earnings into the business to finance expansion on strictly a pay-as-you-go basis. It was a period of emergence: maximum consolidation of functions, tighter check on inventories, check-and-balance control of store costs. Central accounting and central payment of store rents were launched. A paid vacation program for employees was inaugurated thereby making Woolworth among the earliest to provide its personnel with that fringe benefit. And the Woolworth Christmas Bonus was started, together with the practice of paying Woolworth store employees higher wages during the Christmas peak season.

So as to comb European markets for such values as were then unavailable to Woolworth's syndicate in domestic markets for sale at Five-and-Ten prices, Frank Woolworth, now liberated by Peck's efficient presence in the New York Office, sailed in February 1890 on his initial European buying trip— on the first of the 44 transatlantic crossings of his lifetime. On that 88-day shopping expedition, he exhausted the marketplaces of England, Germany, Austria and France.

Sailing on the crack liner S.S. *City of Paris,* which then held the transatlantic speed record, Queenstown to New York, Woolworth, through almost daily General Letters sent to the New York Office for processing and dissemination, thereafter created a tight log of his travels, doings and impressions that kept his executives and managers agog with interest. A few examples follow.

Passages from his shipboard notes included:

The agony is over and my dear friends who came to see me off have just gone home; and we are left to the mercy of the elements. . . . The sea is black and ugly and the ship rolls and pitches. Pulled on my waterproof ulster and managed to get up on deck. It was the grandest sight I ever saw. The waves were mountains high, fifty feet I should say by actual measurement. These great waves toss our ship about as if it was made of cork. . . . We just passed Fastnet Light and are in the Irish Sea. Everything is calm and my sickness is gone. Have forgotten how sick I was already.

Upon landing in England, Woolworth rushed to pottery country in search for chinaware. From Stokes on Trent, he wrote, in part:

I can eat now and never was so hungry in my life. This is the centre of the potteries, over 600 of them in the County of Staffordshire. Some of the finest china in the world is made here and some of the poorest. We have been in over 25 potteries in the last three days and have not bought anything yet, but expect to next week. . . .

We went today to a hotel for dinner and ate in what they call "The Ordinary." It cost us two-and-three-pence [then about 56 cents], and is patronized mostly by commercial men or travelers. The first thing they do is elect a President who must be the oldest patron of the hotel, not in age but according to the length of time he has stopped there. He sits at the head of the table and is the carver, and the Vice-President sits at the foot of the table and is his assistant carver. Today there were 16 at the table.

First they brought on the soup, and then about 50 pounds of roast beef, and set it before the President; and some roast mutton, and placed it before the Vice President. . . . When all were ready, the President said to the Vice: "Mr. Vice, will you assist me in serving the gentlemen?" Vice responded "yes," then they got down to business. The roast beef was the finest I ever ate. After that course was over, they served puddings in the same way, and then cheese as Englishmen nearly always finish up on cheese. After all were through, the waiter came around with a silver plate and collected the two shillings, three pence, commencing with the President, after which the President thanked us very kindly and all was over. It is a very nice custom and I wonder it has never been introduced in America.

Proceeding next to London, the Chief was first taken aback by its smoke and soot, then fell victim to its abundant charms. He penned his impressions, and at least two were to influence large later undertakings of his:

.... The stores themselves are very small and are called "shops" and not much like our fine stores. I think a good penny and six pence store run by a live Yankee would create a sensation here, but perhaps not. . . . This forenoon we spent buying goods such as scrap books, albums, etc. and took lunch in a restaurant in the Old Palace of Richard the Third, in its Throne Room. The bill of fare was dated 1466 but the meats and vegetables were comparatively modern. We then visited the Houses of Parliament, or at least looked at them from outside. And Westminster Abbey I consider one of the greatest sights in London. . . . They were holding services at the time and we had a chance to hear the Great Organ, and I never heard such a fine-tone organ before. . . .

Traveling with the veteran European buyer of a large New York importing corporation, Woolworth next crossed the North Sea into Holland, then journeyed to Cologne and Frankfurt in Germany. Sonneberg came next.

Sonneberg is headquarters for dolls for the whole world, as nearly every doll of every description is made here or within a few miles from here, and this is the market. It is a place of about 15,000 people. . . . It seems as though the whole toy trade of America is represented here.

. . . . It is no longer a mystery to me how they make dolls and toys so cheap, for most of it is done by women and children at their homes within 20 miles of this place. Some of the women of America think they have got hard work to do, but it is different than the poor women here, who work night and day on toys, and strap them on their backs, and go 10 or 20 miles through the mud with 75 pounds on their back, to sell them. The usual price they get for a good 10¢ doll is about 3¢ here, and they are obliged to buy the hair, shirts and other materials, to put them together. . . . They probably get about 1¢ each for the labor they put in them. . . .

While in Sonneberg, the Chief made some precious marketing discoveries, and also learned caution in venturing into a foreign language in which he was not, at this stage, fluent.

We can find out more about the toy and china business of America here than at home. Here we find out what the other firms are buying and what they pay for the goods. I have found out where those Sailor Dolls that we sold so many of are made here, and we can save considerable by buying them direct. We have also struck a firm where a certain house in Philadelphia gets a big line of toys that we have bought for several years. Nearly all dealers on this side tell us whom they sell in America. I am trying to learn German but it is a very hard language to learn. . . . I came very near being thrown out of a window in one sample room while I was trying to test my German, and mistakenly told a man he was no good without knowing the meaning. Since then, I have been very, very careful. They all have great sport with me trying to learn, but I don't care, but keep at it every day. . . .

In the mountainside hamlet of Lauscha, tiny in size, large then in output of marbles and tree decorations, probably nonexistent as an entity today, Woolworth, for the first time, saw marbles and Christmas tree ornaments home-produced by the families of that wee Thuringian community. "We waded through ankle-deep mud, uphill and down, all day," he wrote. But the rugged house-to-house expedition paid off in well-worth "buys."

Journeying, midst sheer scenic beauty, to snow-covered Gotha nestled atop a mountain of Saxony, the Chief next explored, with evidently favorable buying result, the sample rooms of the world's largest manufacturers of toy tea sets centered there. Then on he went to Nuremberg, a mecca for toys (years later, site of the World War II Crimes trials)—on, next, to charming Munich (locale, over eight decades later, of the unforgettable XX Olympiad)—then to Vienna, Austrian capital with which he fell instantly and head-over-heels in love. He wrote, in part:

> Vienna, beautiful, magnificent, words cannot express the beauties of this city. . . . Such artistic and fine buildings all over the city, such fine statuary on every side, such fine carvings, such works of art, must be seen to be appreciated. . . . The store windows make the finest display of any city I was ever in. "The Graba" is the great retail street and is thronged continually from 8 A.M. to 8 P.M. The proper time for ladies ["handsomest in the world" he called them] to go shopping is between 4 P.M. and 8 P.M., and that is the time to see the people. . . .
>
> In the afternoon [Good Friday, April 1890], I took a drive out of the city to the Emperor's Summer Palace. . . . In the Emperor's bedroom, saw the original bed that Napoleon I slept in when he occupied the Palace after he had taken the city. He must have been a perfect terror to all of Europe in his time, as we see his works nearly every place we go. . . .
>
> Today being Easter Sunday, visited several churches and the music was grand to hear. Every church has a regular orchestra and large chimes. Saw the Emperor himself [Emperor-King Francis Joseph I] pass in his carriage. . . . Oh, I wish I could stay here longer, but no use, I must go tonight sure. . . .

He then hurried to Leipzig for that city's world-famed annual Leipzig Fair. About his experience, he wrote, in part:

> Get out of the way, hustle up, tumble up, confusion. That is Leipsig during the Fair. Leipsig is a city of 150,000 but now there are over 100,000 strangers here. They call it a Fair but it is not like our Fairs. Thousands of manufacturers from all over the world rent rooms as near the heart of the city as possible, at very high prices, and bring samples of their goods here for sale. . . . If anyone likes hard work and lots of it, come here and look over samples all day. . . . While in Sonneberg I gave a large order for Christmas tree ornaments and I am pointed out on every corner of the street as the big buyer of tree ornaments, and they tackle me everywhere trying to sell me more. . . .

An avalanche of mail greeted the Chief upon his arrival in Berlin and, in his next General Letter, he said, in part:

> Sales I see are all ahead of last year. Mr. Peck has grasped the situation very quickly, and taken my place in the New York Office in fine shape. When reading these long letters [General Letters], don't forget the immense amount of work it makes Miss Holahan in reading my miserable writing and copying them for you with Mr. Ivie's help. . . . They have been written on the cars, by candlelight, and under all circumstances, whenever I could catch a moment's time. . . . This afternoon Mr. Hunt and I took a walk on the "Unter Den Linden." We heard a great commotion, and rolling of drums, and soldiers presenting arms, and thousands of people rushing to the centre of the street, and a fine carriage coming at full speed drawn by four elegant horses, and plumes, and footmen in fine livery, and, in the carriage, was the Emperor himself seated by the side of a lady. He [Deutscher Kaiser Wilhelm II] is very young looking and had on a brass helmet and fine uniform. It was a sight to see people take off their hats and bow. . . . Tonight we go to see Verdi's new opera, "Othello." . . .

En route to Paris, Woolworth's interest was aroused by the heated debate, in French, of several Frenchmen seated near him on that Berlin–Paris train. "I listened very attentively," he wrote, "and managed to learn one very important word, 'Oui,' pronounced 'wee,' which means 'yes' in French." Thus well-equipped, he came face-to-face with the renowned French capital for the first time. Some excerpts from his log include:

The more one sees of Paris, the more magnificent it looks and there seems to be no limit to its grandeur. . . . The cabs here are very cheap. You can ride anywhere for one-and-a-half francs [then about 30 cents] but the driver will call out "Poor Boy" [pourboire] which in English means a tip. . . . Today, visited the Luxemburg and I enjoyed the modern paintings and the statuary more than the old ones at the Louvre. Saw the Pantheon and rode up the famous boulevard Champs-Elysees to the Arc de Triomphe and saw Napoleon's Tomb. . . .

This afternoon I visited the world-famous store "The Bon Marche" which is probably the largest store in the world. They employ 4,000 people regularly and feed them all in the same building. It is as much like the Wanamaker's store in Phila-delphia as any store I know of, but on a much larger scale. On its busy days, its sales can total up to 1,500,000 francs [then about $300,000]. They use no cash system whatsoever, but each customer must go to the desk and pay for what they buy. . . .

Last night went to the opera "Faust." The Opera House itself is indescribably beautiful. . . . While in the Cathedral of Notre Dame, heard the large organ and some very fine singing. . . . All the words I now know in French are "yes," "no," "waiter" and "thank you." I can also count to twelve. . . .

Having completed his business in Paris during that memo-rable week, the Chief then sadly crossed back to England, re-visited the potteries and checked the status of his prior orders, then finalized his affairs in London. He sailed for home from Liverpool on May 10 aboard the S.S. *Etruria*. While the ship stopped in Queenstown en route to New York, her cabin passengers were given opportunity to visit ashore. The Chief and three of his shipboard companions were among the first to lay foot on Irish soil. He wrote, in part:

> Four of us got into a jaunting cart to see the town. This is rightly named. We hung on with all our might while the driver whipped up his horse and cracked jokes for us, which he seemed to be as full of as a nut of meat. I asked him if he knew my Grandfather [Henry McBrier, his maternal grandfather] when he lived in Ireland [he emigrated in 1827]. "Oh yes, I knew him well," he said. "He was a foine man with strait hair, curley teeth and only one upper lip."

The *Etruria* landed Woolworth in New York on Sunday, May 18, and on that very day, he penned the concluding installment of his General Letter travelogue. He wrote, in part:

> "Home Sweet Home" at last. It's almost worth the three month's trip for the pleasure of this day alone. . . . Such hugging and kissing I never got before. The only duty that I had to pay was for three big dolls I got for my children. . . . As soon as I landed, I asked Mr. Kirby [Fred M. Kirby] where my brother was. And the reply was that he had been very busy in the past week and had succeeded in raising an 8-pound boy. . . . Everything seemed to run smooth under Mr. Peck. Before concluding, I want to thank Mr. Ivie, my bookkeeper, and Miss Holahan, the typewriter [secretary, circa 1890], for the way they have copied and mailed my letters. I have tried to explain Europe as it looked to me. . . .

Thereafter, a veritable torrent of values flowed from European warehouses and factories to Woolworth counters for sale to amazed American consumers at nickel-and-dime prices:

china, for instance, from the potteries of England; dolls from Sonneberg, then world's doll capital; marbles from Lauscha; vases and glass goods from Bohemia; Christmas tree decorations from Thuringia; spectacular buys from the Leipzig Fair and other European bazaars. In time, in fact, Woolworth buyers were shuttling to and from world markets, and world products were flowing into America's Main Streets at Woolworth prices.

Consumer reaction to the results of the Chief's first foreign shopping exercise is exemplified by the following letter from Mrs. A. C. Coons, majesty of Woolworth Syracuse, that Woolworth spread into his July 18, 1890, General Letter:

> When I came in sight of the store this morning, I remembered those stories that Mr. Moore told us of throngs battering down prisoners' doors, and I thought to myself, "I was there." I got in through the back door and opened the front door. There was no use trying to form a line. It was a riot!
>
> I sent for a policeman. No sooner did he gaze upon those beautiful things than he was overcome and joined the melee. So this gray-haired lady formed herself into a police force and tried to keep the crowd from killing the clerks and smashing plate glass. As I write, the store is jammed.

The landed cost of Woolworth European purchases ballooned from $500,000 in 1896 to over $2 million in 1907. Nevertheless, the preponderance of Woolworth merchandise was bought American, as American manufacturers first reluctantly accepted, then eagerly and aggressively courted, Woolworth's large-quantity, for cash, direct purchases. Notwithstanding vast foreign importing, for example, over 80 percent of the merchandise bought by the company for resale over its counters in 1900 was purchased from American sources. Parenthetically it can be added that the American ratio rose to 86 percent by 1908, to about 99.5 percent by 1939.

Consumer Acceptance Woolworth's Hallmark

Woolworth was a pathfinder in consumer acceptance. As a purchasing agent of the consumer, he allowed himself to be governed, from the start, by the needs and wants of his stores' patrons.

He recognized at Lancaster, and thereafter, the importance of diversification of merchandise. Accordingly, he increasingly supplemented his "bread-and-butter" stock of goods with surprise additions such as novelty, fad and style goods desired by his customers.

He made a wide variety of seasonal merchandise attractively available to his stores' traffic when most wanted—Christmas, Thanksgiving, Easter, the full range.

Woolworth stores were distinctive in convenience, orderliness and attractive appearance in the early Nineties, and became ever larger and ever more impressive even before the century turned.

He put his stock out where people could see and examine it. With merchandise conspicuously displayed on increasingly modern counters, plainly marked, consumers were encouraged to browse around the store undisturbed, and to buy or not depending upon their own bent. Hence, more and more people viewed visiting the Woolworth "red-front" substantially as they regarded going to a fair. And when they browsed Woolworth, many bought on sheer impulse.

Woolworth frowned upon coercive selling. Strong-arm methods offended him. The girl behind the counter was there to complete the sale, not to initiate it. Customers had to learn for themselves that because Woolworth goods were inexpensive did not mean that they were cheap.

He sought the patronage of the old and the young. He was among the first merchants, perhaps even the first, to cater systematically to children. The year-round toy values offered in Woolworth stores in the Nineties and thereafter were, in their day, considered sensational.

Just as Woolworth popularized Christmas tree ornamentation by introducing Christmas tree decorations to America at nickel-and-dime prices, so too did he make good candy available to consumers at Woolworth prices in a day when some producers told him that candy acceptable to him couldn't even be made, much less retailed, at 5¢ per quarter-pound.

In the high-sugar-price days of 1887 when candy fit to eat seldom cost less than 40¢ per pound and was, in effect, a luxury primarily enjoyed by those able to afford it, the Chief, with William Moore in tow, unsuccessfully confronted one New York candy manufacturer after another in search for breakthrough. Finally the twosome found its way to D. Arnould's small candy establishment on Wooster Street in downtown Manhattan. And Mr. Arnould listened attentively as Woolworth spelled out his plan.

"We talked with Mr. Arnould in regard to our project," Woolworth recounted years later, "and he got very enthusiastic and said that he would get up a line of goods. . . . He told us to call again in a couple of days. We did and we had about 20 items that we could sell at the price of a quarter-pound for 5¢." The Chief immediately ordered 500 pounds to be shipped, 100 pounds per store, to the five Woolworth stores that he picked for the candy test.

He set a Saturday forenoon as the zero hour for the simultaneous launching of the candy experiment in the five picked "red-fronts." To each he rushed scales, glass trays, scoops and a quantity of bags, together with precise instructions as to candy display and candy sales technique to be used.

His "partner-managers" of 1887 "kicked" at the very idea of trying to sell candy in a Five-and-Ten. They "kicked" hard, they "kicked" unanimously. Woolworth, however, stood firm.

The project proceeded on schedule as planned. And when all five stores experienced a consumer run on candy, erstwhile "kicks" changed to enthusiasm and high favor.

Eventually, candy became a superstar in Woolworth's line. And Mr. Arnould garnered so many and such large candy orders from the Woolworth syndicate that he had to erect a large factory on Canal Street, New York, to accommodate demand.

In 1897, Woolworth "red-fronts" sold about 4 million pounds of quality candy in that single year. Two decades later, 90 million pounds were annually being sold, meaning enough to fill a train of freight cars 24 miles long.

"Red-Fronts" for East's Big Cities

Frank Woolworth made a sweeping, in-depth feasibility study of the qualifications and growth potential of his surging syndicate in 1895, and was confident that the Woolworth Five-and-Ten was now ready to enter the East's really big cities and engage their big-league stores in one-on-one combat for in-store traffic. He had the cash, moreover, to equip his market entries so as to meet almost any competition. Step by step, therefore, he entered Newark, New Jersey, then Jersey City, New Jersey, then Washington, D.C., that year. And that autumn, Woolworth reached Brooklyn, New York, then an autonomous municipality of nearly a million people.

Located on Fulton Street near Flatbush Avenue, in the very heart of the city's premier shopping district, Woolworth's "red-front" opened for business on November 6, 1895, just six months before the enactment of the Greater New York Act that, effective January 1, 1898, made Brooklyn one of New York's five boroughs. Throngs welcomed the premiering "beauty." And traffic's reaction to that emporium's elegance inspired the Chief to undertake the store enlargement and beautification program that revolutionized the visage of Woolworth "red-fronts" of that era. He himself said:

> The first fixtures that we put into the Brooklyn store in the Fall of 1895 were so far superior to the fixtures of any of our other stores, and our trade was so tremendous, that we decided to introduce these fine fixtures in all the stores opened after that date.
>
> All stores opened since that date have modern and beautiful fixtures, and the old fixtures have been thrown out of the older stores and modern ones substituted. This has been one of the reasons why our trade has since increased at such a rate.

On the heels of the Brooklyn store's debut came the openings of large Woolworth stores in Philadelphia, then Boston. These set stage for the "great advent"—the arrival of the "red-front" in New York itself. Woolworth's dream of Manhattan entry was actually fulfilled on October 31, 1896, in the heat of the William McKinley–William Jennings Bryan presidential campaign.

The Empire City's great stores of that day were mainly concentrated in the rectangular area between 14th and 23rd Streets, and between Sixth Avenue and Broadway. That late October day, Woolworth opened his 33rd store, by far his largest, his first two-story Five-and-Ten, on Sixth Avenue between 16th and 17th Streets. Center and overhead on that crowded avenue ran the tracks upon which rumbled the busy trains of the Sixth Avenue elevated railroad. Parades and other presidential-campaign distractions drew masses of people. But the Woolworth "red-front" drew huge in-store traffic nonetheless.

Manhattan's shoppers embraced that "red-front" so close to bosom that, four years almost to the day after its 1896 opening, it was succeeded by a Five-and-Ten "colossus" erected directly across the street. Occupying 12,000 square feet of floor space and hailed as the "world's largest Five-and-Ten," that new store introduced consumers to new luxuries in store environment. An expensive, in-store pipe organ, for example, serenaded customers with mood music while they browsed and shopped Woolworth. That organ, Woolworth announced, "will remain in this store permanently to discourse classical and sentimental music."

The birth of Woolworth's distinctive pre-opening public "store inspection" or "reception" coincided with the launching of Woolworth's Eastern big-city emporiums. These super Five-and-Tens of that particular era were introduced to their publics with almost the flourish of a debutante's presentation.

Held on the Friday evening prior to their customary Saturday debut of that day, the "inspection" or "reception" was the scene of the resplendent store's welcome to its prospective customers. An orchestra played. There were other attractions; in some cases, other entertainment. Crowds thronged the store's aisles inspecting the values that they would rush to buy on the morrow. The storeful of fresh flowers would later be rushed to the hospitals of the community with the store's compliments.

Frank Woolworth, as seen, stepped into the 1890's with a dozen small stores and with a sales volume for 1889 of $246,782. He entered the twentieth century in 1900 with 54 large, but not yet really huge, stores, judged by 1972 standards. His syndicate's sales volume for 1899 aggregated nearly $4.5 million. He was living his dream. The Woolworth Five-and-Ten had come of age.

When his Lancaster "mother" store opened in June 1879, it carried this $410 inventory of "Yankee Notions":

Skimmers	Fire shovels	Cover lifters
Purses	Toy dustpans	Writing books
Ladles	Drinking cups	Pencil charms
Graters	Animal soap	Tack hammers

Baseballs	Candlesticks	Lather brushes
Egg whips	Apple corers	Cake cutters
Tin scoops	Cake tins	Cake turners
ABC plates	Boot blacking	Biscuit cutters
Pie plates	School straps	Gravy strainers
Tack claws	Flour dredges	Tin pepper boxes

As the Woolworth syndicate turned the century, its 54 "red-fronts" carried:

Candy	Pictures	Rubber goods
Jewelry	Perfumery	Handkerchiefs
Soap	Novelties	Foreign china
Novels	Glassware	Drug sundries
Frames	Knit goods	Leather goods
Ribbons	Wire goods	Greeting cards
Brushes	Dry goods	Japanese goods
Mirrors	Toys, dolls	Millinery goods
Tinware	Silverware	Celluloid goods
Baskets	Stoneware	Christmas tree
Notions	Yellowware	decorations
Hosiery	Enamelware	Foreign crockery
Hardware	Woodenware	American crockery
Stationery		

Inordinate "buys" that too had already made their appearance on Woolworth counters included: moustache cups, fountain pens, envelopes, flowerpots, paraffin candles, boxes of candy, crepe paper, suspenders and belts, enamel ironware, playing cards, tooth powder, talcum, spectacles, among others —all offered at nickel-and-dime prices in an otherwise high-retail-price day.

Even a grocery line had been launched in 1897. Packed for Woolworth's Diamond W Pure Food Company by a leading grocery manufacturer, the line was store-tested in Albany, Boston, New York, Washington and Brooklyn, then extended to some additional "red-fronts." The experiment was halted, however, in 1899.

Woolworth Burgeons as Century Turns

The nation briskly turned the century with a population of 76 million that would swell to 92 million within another decade. Markets were now national. The Machine Age had begun. The powerful propulsion of the Industrial Revolution was accelerating the momentum of American industry. Labor-saving machines that the engineers had been developing for a quarter-century were now making their first records in mass production, not very impressive records, to be sure, judged by later standards, but substantial enough to demand the development of a system of large-scale distribution to team with large-scale production.

Roads were developed at a relatively fast pace during this post-1900 decade. The automobile came. And its development and increasing use helped to broaden the trade areas of enlarging municipalities. More and more people from farms and small towns consequently came to neighboring larger communities to shop for a wider range of consumer goods. In cities, ethnic enclaves flourished as immigration boomed.

Newspaper circulation's expansion stimulated the infant field of advertising to grow in the scheme of marketing, thereby sharpening consumer appetite. Advent of rural free delivery of the mail generated the progress of countrywide mail-order selling. Accordingly, Sears Roebuck and Montgomery Ward, and their mail-order catalogues, soon became household names in city and village though neither had, as yet, opened a single retail store.

With more mouths to feed, more bodies to clothe, more feet to be shoed, consumer goods manufacturers were now able to produce ever larger output of consumer-wanted merchandise in that period's buyers' market. Their need was to unload products of their growing capacity faster, profitably. Unlike earlier day, the mass producer increasingly courted the large-scale retail distributor. Mass production and consumer demand, consequently, contributed prime challenge and opportunity to existent multi-unit retail distributors, so-called chain stores, to accelerate their expansion. Moreover, they influenced the growth of many effective "starting" stores to multi-unit status.

F. W. Woolworth's steadily escalating syndicate of Five-and-Tens, and The Great Atlantic & Pacific Tea Company in the grocery field, were already the nation's chain-store giants as the twentieth century dawned.

Founded by George F. Gilman as The Great American Tea Company in 1859, and developed by George Huntington Hartford as The Great Atlantic & Pacific Tea Company, the A & P operated nearly 200 stores in 28 states in 1901. F. W. Woolworth headed a network of 60 larger, higher-volume "red-fronts" that same year. By the standards of that time, both pioneer chains already had vast and growing buying and selling power to offer large-scale sources of supply, to the consumers' benefit. And other well-established chains were also on the firing line.

Five-and-Ten syndicates started with single stores by S. H. Knox (1889), F. M. Kirby (1887), C. S. Woolworth (1883), S. S. Kresge (1897), S. H. Kress (1896) and J. G. McCrory (1881) had made substantial headway on America's Main Streets by 1901, and were headed forward. Chain-store companies in other fields, already successful and expanding, were Grand-Union Co. (1872), Kroger Grocery & Baking Co. (1882), National Tea Co. (1899), G. R. Kinney Co. (1894), Jewel Tea Co. (1899), and, among others, the ancestor companies from which American Stores Co. (1887)

and First National Stores, Inc. (1895) respectively stemmed.

Just around the corner as the 1900's dawned, moreover, was the creation, from single store beginnings, of J. C. Penney Co. (1902), W. T. Grant Co. (1906), United Cigar Co. (1901), Liggett Drug Co. (1907), Walgreen Drug Company (1906), Western Auto Supply Co. (1909), G. C. Murphy Co. (1901), J. J. Newberry Co. (1912), Safeway Stores, Inc. (1915), and others that became prominent chain-store corporations.

There was substantial mutual benefit derivable from the wedding of mass production and mass distribution. Woolworth's large cash orders, for instance, were generally placed with manufacturers long enough in advance to permit such producers to buy raw materials in quantity at a saving. They enabled the producer to reduce his overhead expenses by standardizing production and by employing economical machine processes.

Huge orders placed direct by Frank Woolworth's syndicate obviated the necessity for extensive promotional and market development outlays by the producer. They stimulated more rapid and regular turnover of his inventories, eliminated the congestion of merchandise in storage, liberated otherwise frozen capital, and assisted in stabilizing employment year-round.

The financial might of Woolworth and the sureness of prompt, cold-cash payment, moreover, freed the manufacturer from the vagaries of credit transaction.

These and other boons altogether enabled the producer to make extraordinary values available to Woolworth for sale in his "red-fronts," in wide-open display, at fixed nickel-and-dime prices. Consumers, consequently, thronged to buy Woolworth.

As the infant new century gained heft, Woolworth counters brimmed with new attractions. The widely wanted books of

Horatio Alger, hero of the American boy of that day, for example, were now on sale in Woolworth Five-and-Tens. Lapel insignia of numerous fraternal, benevolent, religious and other societies, lodges, associations and orders were being offered on his counters. With the approval of His Eminence Cardinal Gibbons of Baltimore, prayer books, scapulars, rosaries and other such denominational objects were now on sale in many Woolworth stores for the accommodation of the faithful.

Ice skates; infants' wear; umbrellas; extra-large goldfish; tumblers inscribed "Father," "Mother," or other such familial designation; flag-shaped pins of colleges; dust goggles; dust caps; brooches with Army or Navy insignia; house signs such as "To Let" or "For Rent"; brooches with the respective crests of England, France, Germany, etc.; these and many other popular goods courted purchase from "red-front" counters.

Sheet music and folios, amazingly, made their first appearance on Woolworth counters at least as early as 1886. And even more surprising was the experiment undertaken in 1890 of selling music by direct mail. But neither sheet music nor folio was a favored sales item among most Woolworth managers of that day. Consequently, they were dropped from the Approved List in 1893 as a result of a managers' poll.

The "Merry Widow Waltz" swept to such heights of popularity a few years later that consumer demand caused Woolworth to stock and sell the sheet music of that gem. Continuing demand for that classic and for a widening number of other titles stimulated the return of sheet music to the Approved List in 1911.

Thereafter, Woolworth's sheet music counters abounded with vocals, galops, rags, reveries, waltzes, two-steps, three-steps and other of that era's music. And they were joined by phonograph records when the Victrola craze swelled to heroic proportions, coast to coast.

In that day before radio, television, the jukebox, and motion pictures synchronized to sound, Woolworth's drawing power and Woolworth's open display, supplemented by in-store demonstrators, doubtlessly did as much to gain popularity for many of the songs that became hits as any other single medium. In a single pre–World War I year alone, for instance, Woolworth units sold 20 million sheets of music and 5 million phonograph records.

Splendor Transforms Mother Store

Frank Woolworth's first Woolworth Building was rising in Lancaster, Pennsylvania, as the twentieth century dawned. Punctuating the 21st anniversary of the birth there of his historic "mother" store, the structure was completed and appropriately dedicated in late autumn of 1900, in the fading afterglow of the nation's gala welcome to the new century.

A handsome five-story-with-roof-garden office building fronting two busy Lancaster streets, the four upper floors were rented to tenants as office quarters. Woolworth, an inveterate and widely sought tenant, now, therefore, became a landlord himself for the very first time.

On the ground floor of that Woolworth Building, he housed a Five-and-Ten that in size, splendor and offered values was a far cry from its tiny but mighty ancestor. The transformation of the "mother" store had become a syndicate labor of love. At the sumptuous reception that occurred on the Friday evening preceding its Saturday business opening, Woolworth and his associates appraisingly looked around them, also took in the obvious enthusiasm of the many browsing Lancastrians, and styled the new emporium "The Gem of the Syndicate."

Six large windows, mirror-paneled and well lighted, wooed the walking traffic of the two streets on which they fronted. The store interior welcomed in-store traffic with wide aisles, the latest in counters and lighting, marble-topped pillars, and paneled green sidewalls decorated with gold leaf.

The Diamond W emblazoned in gold occupied one of those sidewall panels. Another listed all extant Woolworth stores. "This is the oldest established 5 and 10 cent store in the world" was the message carried by another. Others respectively proclaimed: "Goods displayed in Woolworth stores are collected from all parts of the world"; "Nothing in this store over 10 cents"; "Large purchases for cash from manufacturers explain the high values we offer"; and finally, "The Woolworth stores require and employ 5,000 people to sell over a million articles annually."

Frank Woolworth, in his lifetime, never lost interest in Lancaster, the beginning point of his career as an effective purchasing agent of the consumer—the community in which, for example, he saw a Christmas tree decorated in the brilliant German manner for the very first time and then proceeded to popularize Christmas tree ornamentation, ultimately becoming the world's largest importer of such decorations. Within less than a dozen years of the 1900 opening of the Lancaster Woolworth Building, it became a towered seven-story edifice with air-cushioned elevators, and the "Gem of the Syndicate" was enlarged, modernized and beautified twice.

Woolworths Sink Fifth Avenue Roots

The turn of the century also marked a milepost in Frank Woolworth's personal life. The Woolworth family moved from Brooklyn Heights to Manhattan.

Consisting of Jennie and himself, and their three lovely daughters—Helena, twenty-two, Edna, seventeen, and Jessie, fourteen—the Woolworths first made their home in the Savoy Hotel on Fifth Avenue, then moved into a 30-room marble mansion on the corner of Fifth Avenue and 80th Street, in the heart of that era's so-called "Millionaires Row," descendant of the opulent Broad Way of yesteryear.

Woolworth's predilection for marble was given expression in the construction of that house. Besides being many, its rooms were spacious and its furnishings and appointments rich. But perhaps the possession that gave Woolworth as much personal pleasure and relaxation as any was the superb pipe organ, a wonder of its time, that he had installed in the drawing room.

A born deep lover of music, even though he neither played an instrument nor could read music, he graduated easily, and with great satisfaction, from his player piano and phonograph that used to delight him by the hour to his new pipe organ that could be played automatically. He collected a treasure of music rolls. He experimented with apparatus producing lighting and effects of sound. Eventually, not only could he concurrently produce excellent music on his organ but also appropriate lighting and sound effects for the music being played.

For several years after moving to that Fifth Avenue town house the Woolworths were a fivesome. Then Helena Woolworth was married in that home in 1904 to Charles E. F. McCann, a young lawyer. Edna became Mrs. Franklyn Laws Hutton in the Church of the Heavenly Rest on Fifth Avenue in 1907. And young Jessie was wed to James Paul Donahue in the Woolworth mansion in 1912. The fivesome thus became a twosome.

Woolworth turned loss into gain. So as to have his daughters and their families close to home, he bought four parcels of land on East 80th Street, contiguous to his Fifth Avenue town house, and built three handsome homes. Hence, the plot of land fronting Fifth Avenue and extending deep into East 80th Street became, in effect, a Woolworth family compound.

As a supplement to the town house, the Woolworths acquired a summer home in the earliest days of World War I. Located in Glen Cove, New York, and commanding a capital view of Long Island Sound, they named it Winfield Hall. But their joy of possession of that home was short-lived. It burned to the ground on November 16, 1916. Again Woolworth turned loss into gain. He immediately called upon Cass Gilbert to build him an Italian Renaissance mansion that would do justice to the beauty of his estate.

From the standpoint of both quality and speed, the eminent architect rose to the occasion. The new Winfield Hall was a storybook three-story palace of white marble. The elegance of its interior achieved wide note, as did the excellence of the estate's nine-hole golf course. Wired for sound, the palace even housed a pipe organ of superior quality.

"Red-Fronts" for America's West

Within four years of the coming of the new century, Frank Woolworth's spreading network swept west. A historic event, in effect, triggered the westward propulsion of the Diamond W.

The hotels of Utica, New York, on Washington's Birthday, 1904, were overflowing with Woolworth executives, buyers, and store managers, who had converged upon the city from ten East Coast states and the District of Columbia to observe the 25th anniversary of the opening of Woolworth's first "Great 5¢ Store."

At the banquet there that evening honoring Frank Woolworth, the program was climaxed by an impressive presentation to the Chief. The morale, confidence and togetherness of his business family, demonstrated to him that evening, touched him deeply.

The very next day, Woolworth, accompanied by two aides, headed west. Within two weeks, he not only inspected and purchased the 14 stores of Pfohl, Smith & Co. but also appraised and bought the three stores of S. D. Rider, the three stores of G. B. Carey, and the single store of John W. Carey. He paid spot cash for these purchased 21 units within two weeks.

About this swift move that first brought Woolworth to Colorado, Illinois, Indiana, Iowa, Minnesota, Missouri, Nebraska, North Dakota and Wisconsin, he said in his General Letter:

> Few of the people assembled at that banquet that night knew exactly what I had in mind for the future of this five and ten cent store business. . . . Most of you now know what has been accomplished as far as extending the business is concerned. . . . It was your encouragement that night that helped me to put more money into the business as you all had faith in it, and so did I. . . .

To facilitate assimilation, administration, supervision and inspection, Woolworth grouped these 21 fledgling "red-fronts" into a so-called Western District. A fully staffed District Office, Woolworth's first, was opened in the Railway Exchange Building, Chicago, that May. To head it, the Chief tapped Charles C. Griswold, a veteran of a decade's Woolworth service and, as seen, Woolworth's first store inspector, now his first District Manager.

Woolworth's planned expansion, furthermore, was not restricted to Westward Ho! In his behalf, Carson Peck journeyed to McKeesport, Pennsylvania, that August and effected the cash purchase of a dozen of G. C. Murphy's 14 Monongahela River valley "dime stores." And later that year, Woolworth bought and absorbed the three Massachusetts units of E. H. Farnsworth, and the single store of A. A. Hughes, a former Woolworth manager, whom he promptly reinstated.

Woolworth operated 76 stores in 10 states and the District of Columbia as the curtain rose on his Silver Anniversary Year in 1904. As a result of the buying and assimilating of those 37 stores, and of the opening of seven Woolworth "redfronts," including entry stores in Kansas and Ohio, the Diamond W linked 120 Five-and-Tens in 21 states and the District of Columbia when the curtain descended that year.

Compared with aggregate sales of $4,415,110 for 1899, Woolworth sales totaled $10,210,000 for 1904. In state concentration, New York and Pennsylvania led with 25 "redfronts" each.

Woolworth Incorporates Woolworth Network

Ill in Switzerland a few years back, Frank Woolworth had wrestled both with pneumonia and with gnawing concern as to what would happen to his business, and to the men and women of his syndicate, were he, its sonless owner, to decease or to become incapacitated. His worry recurred intermittently, grew greater with recurrence.

Early in 1905, following months of consultation and planning, he attacked his problem head-on. He transformed the structure of his syndicate from an unincorporated company, wholly owned by himself, to a corporation, controlled and headed by himself, organized under the laws of the State of New York. Its name: F. W. Woolworth & Co., Inc.

"Did any of the managers ever stop to think what would have become of the business should anything serious have happened to me?" Woolworth asked in his General Letter of February 28, 1905, that announced the incorporation.

"Now," he said, "every manager in every store, every clerk and every office boy, every manager of the New York and

Chicago offices, is on a safe basis. . . . No matter what happens to me as President, or to any of the other officers of the company, the business goes on just the same."

Incorporated on February 14, 1905, F. W. Woolworth & Co. had authorized, issued and outstanding capital stock totaling $10 million. This amount was represented by 100,000 shares, each of the par value of $100, of which $5 million was 7% cumulative preferred stock, and $5 million was common stock. The common stock carried sole voting power so long as preferred stock dividends, payable quarterly, were disbursed when due and payable. Parenthetically, it can be added in passing that, without a single delay or omission, such preferred stock dividends were paid throughout the life of that corporation.

Aside from F. W. Woolworth, President, the infant company's officers included Carson C. Peck and Clinton Pierce Case as Vice-Presidents, Hubert T. Parson as Secretary-Treasurer, and Charles C. Griswold and H. W. Cowan as Assistant Treasurers. Woolworth, Peck, Case, Parson and Harry A. Moody composed the young corporation's first Board of Directors.

Mineola, Long Island, became the site of the company's statutory Principal Office. But its imposing headquarters in the Stewart Building remained its Executive Office.

Woolworth, who had transferred full ownership of his syndicate to F. W. Woolworth & Co. in return for all of that corporation's authorized, issued and outstanding capital stock, then offered common stock at par to all company officers, buyers, and inspectors. He offered preferred stock at par, moreover, to all of the foregoing plus Woolworth store managers.

The rush by Woolworth men and women to purchase stock staggered Woolworth, who interpreted the stampede as visible proof of confidence. "It is a source of great satisfaction to me to think," he wrote, "that so many managers are willing to put up their money in a business of this kind, and this is certainly a compliment to me to think that I have so many loyal associates."

Except that F. W. Woolworth & Co. was now a corporation instead of an individually owned business, except that personnel contracts were now with the company instead of with Mr. Woolworth personally, there was no visible difference in Woolworth company operation under the continuing leadership and control of its founder and bellwether.

Within three years, the larger stature that F. W. Woolworth & Co. had already achieved necessitated regionalization of stores for even more effective administration and inspection. Accordingly, all units were grouped, according to geographic location, into six inspection districts. The Boston, Albany, New York and Philadelphia districts reported to the New York Office. The Chicago and Omaha districts reported to the Chicago Office. Each was headed by a District Superintendent, each of whom had climbed the Woolworth ladder by competitively demonstrating qualifications. With the addition of Pittsburgh, Trenton, South Bend and Worcester, the number of districts rose to ten by 1911.

Innovations continued to abound as Woolworth, with tight grip at the helm, pursued progress. As early as 1900 he had scrapped the old Lamson Cable Cash System and had replaced it with cash registers in all stores. In 1909 he scrapped shelves back of counters. He launched a light-lunch-and-soda-pop counter in the Market Street store in Philadelphia in 1907, forerunner of today's Woolworth soda fountains, then added others as their consumer acceptance demanded. The first actual Woolworth lunchroom, ancestor of this day's prepared food service, was opened in the 14th Street store, New York, in 1910.

A year later, Woolworth's Lancaster "mother store," the

then so-called "Gem of the Syndicate," was enlarged and modernized. Impressive addition was its "Refreshment Room"—an elegant lunchroom serving prepared food at nickel-and-dime prices. Its walls and serving counters were of matched marble. Its mahogany tables were topped by Carrara marble. It comfortably accommodated 102 patrons and had a staff of 28.

On the October Saturday, 1911, that it auspiciously opened, 3,279 Woolworth shoppers were served the complete meals of their choice without charge—with the compliments of Woolworth. And the store manager, reporting on the Refreshment Room's subsequent operating performance, had this to say:

> We already have the reputation of serving the best coffee and fried oysters in town. Last Saturday, we served 4,500 oysters. One man ate 26. . . . An old woman looked up from her plate the other day, and stopped eating oysters long enough to say, "Isn't this grand!" She couldn't say any more, but a smile across her face spoke louder than words. . . .
>
> You can still hear people talking about us on the streets and in the trolleys. . . . Every stranger that comes to town is either brought in or comes in of his own accord. . . . One gentleman handed me his card and said, "My wife and I stopped off coming from Harrisburg so as to see this lunch room. . . ."

The arresting power of Woolworth "red-fronts" not only attracted people to their own interiors to browse and buy, but also stimulated traffic beneficial to neighboring retail establishments of all kinds. This was one of many reasons why more and more chambers of commerce and trade boards were soliciting Woolworth to open stores in their respective communities. These requests were usually buttressed by petitions of consumers themselves. The appeal of the housewives of

Andover, Massachusetts, as one example, carried the signatures of over a thousand petitioners.

In the very first census of customers ever made by Woolworth, it was found, by actual clocking, that 1,137,449 consumers entered 170 Woolworth "red-fronts" in 23 states and the District of Columbia on a single day, namely Saturday, May 25, 1907. And it was found that 82 percent of the men, women and children who entered a "red-front" that day to browse or buy actually made a purchase or more.

"Red-Fronts" Dot Britannia's Cities

The Woolworth Five-and-Ten crossed the Atlantic in 1909. But Woolworth's thinking and planning for its migration to Britannia started long before that.

Back in 1890, when Woolworth was in England on his first buying trip, he wrote, "I think that a good 'penny-and-sixpence' run by a live Yankee would create a sensation here. . . ." He then laid the idea aside to gestate.

Revived by a visiting Member of Parliament's inquiry as to the prospect of importing Woolworth "red-fronts" to England, the idea was reexamined in 1898. Mr. Woolworth, however, was still not ready to act.

But in 1909, he was set to go. By early May of that year, he had not only successfully piloted his plan to launch Woolworth "Three-and-Sixpence" stores in England past his Board of Directors but also had picked and prepared three so-called "Volunteer-Pioneers," each a seasoned Woolworth merchant, to spearhead the project in England under his supervision.

Fred Moore Woolworth, the Chief's third cousin and manager of the Sixth Avenue, New York, store, Byron De Witt Miller, Superintendent of the Boston District (and years later, a Woolworth President), and Samuel R. Balfour, manager of the 14th Street, New York, store were his chosen and readied "Volunteer-Pioneers." With their families, together with Mr. and Mrs. Woolworth and young Jessie, they sailed for England on the S.S. *Kaiserin Auguste Victoria* late that May. About these Argonauts, Woolworth wrote in his General Letter:

> . . . These three gentlemen are burning their bridges behind them, and they expect to make England their permanent home. . . . I shall do what I can to help them get these stores started. F. W. Woolworth & Co. will own controlling interest in the company (to be formed in England) but it remains for these three gentlemen to determine whether the business will be a success or failure.

F. W. Woolworth & Co. Limited was incorporated as a private limited company on July 23, 1909, capitalized at £50,250 (then about $250,000). Its capital totaled 10,000 shares, of which 5,000 were preference (preferred) stock at £10 per share, and 5,000 ordinary (common) stock at 1s per share. Two-fifths of that capital was immediately put up in cash. Fred Woolworth was named Managing Director. The three "Volunteer-Pioners" and Frank Woolworth himself comprised the company's first Board of Directors. The only authorized director's fee was £1 per annum (then about $5) for Frank Woolworth. A board member till his death, Mr. Woolworth gleefully claimed that remuneration in gold as long as he lived.

About the impediments, particularly the shallow size of available locations, that immediately faced the pioneering team, the Chief wrote:

> We have discovered why the stores run so shallow here. Customers mostly do their shopping from the store windows. . . . The minute a customer goes into a store, he is met by a floorwalker who wants to know what is wanted, and he is

expected to buy before leaving. . . . The American idea of going into a store to look around without any intention to buy is not practiced here . . . all of which discourages shopping inside the store. . . .

In the center of Liverpool's leading retail district, the "Volunteer-Pioneers" finally found and rented Woolworth's first store in England that August. Formerly an exclusive millinery establishment, the four-story building's three lower floors were fashioned into Woolworth-type sales floors, including a restaurant (styled "Refreshment Room") on the second floor. The first Executive Office of British Woolworth was located on the top floor.

The "Volunteer-Pioneers" were supplemented by a Briton, William Lawrence Stephenson, shortly after their arrival in England. Stephenson, twenty-nine, who then began a Woolworth career that lasted some 40 years, including some 17 later years as a distinguished Chairman of the Board of British Woolworth, had previously met Mr. Woolworth and was remembered by him.

Some years before, Stephenson, then associated with the export merchants Edward Owen & Co., Ltd., of Birmingham, had waited well upon Mr. Woolworth and Clinton Case in Owen's sample room. As the Chief prepared to leave, he placed a hand on the young man's shoulder and said, "Thanks, young man. Some day you'll be a great merchant."

The young Briton never forgot that kindly and encouraging act. As to its aftermath, Stephenson wrote:

A wire came to my office to join them at dinner at Liverpool that evening. I caught a train and went up expecting to book some further orders for merchandise . . . but we just had a pleasant evening together. Thanking me for coming, Mr. Woolworth then asked if I was joining them. I pointed out that this was the first I had heard of it, and asked some reasonable questions. The only answer I received was that he could not tell me. If the effort was a flop, I had lost out; if it was a go, he was in the habit of taking care of his men. . . . Here I had the benefit of my knowledge of Woolworth men and their attitude toward their Chief, and I, therefore, did not hesitate to accept his simple words. . . .

Resplendent in pre-opening-day "inspection" finery, with gala atmosphere set by the music of an eight-piece orchestra, the first Woolworth Three-and-Six opened with a public reception on Friday, November 5, 1909, and for business the following day. Its counters brimmed with alarm clocks, 24-inch handsaws, men's woolen underwear, galvanized buckets, and a storeful of other such unheard of values at 3d. and 6d. prices. Curious but cautious, the local press was on hand. The exhausted "Volunteer-Pioneers," now an Anglo-American foursome, assessed the over-all scene and agreed that British Woolworth was now, at last, set to go.

The public that came in teeming numbers on Friday to look, returned on Saturday to buy. "There was a frenzy of purchasing," Stephenson wrote. "Counterhands were almost shoulder-to-shoulder. Replacements were streaming from stock to sales counter all day. It was evidence that we were offering something to the public that it liked and never before had."

Sales continued steadily brisk day after day. Essentially, however, the enterprise faced one obstacle to complete success as a Woolworth-type, fast-turnover gem. The hurdle was the average Briton's unwillingness to enter a store until he had made selection from the window display, a hallowed British practice counter to Woolworth's hallowed "browsers wanted" policy.

So as to erode, then destroy, that British shopping habit, the "Volunteer-Pioneers" exploited another British habit, the Briton's custom of taking afternoon tea. The "mother" store started serving afternoon tea in its second-floor "Refreshment Room." It served it free for a very long time, then at fixed, very low price, for excellent tea. The practice suited am ·zed consumers fine. And while in the store, they browsed to heart's content and liked it. And they became adept at impulse buying. Britain took British Woolworth close to heart.

Buying mainly British, employing Britons almost entirely, financing its step-by-step development wholly from its own earnings, British Woolworth, within the next decade, grew to a network of 81 popular "three-and-sixes." The first Woolworth store to enter London itself was opened there in April 1913. Launched in Cardiff, the initial Woolworth "red-front" in Wales arrived there in 1913. The first such store in Ireland was opened in Dublin in April 1914. The pioneer Woolworth unit in Scotland had its premiere in Glasgow in October 1914.

American Woolworth, of course, controlled British Woolworth, owning 62 percent of its capital stock then. It still controls it, owning 52.7 percent of its capital stock since 1931, when the British corporation became a public company. But British Woolworth is deeply ingrained British.

So fully did the Woolworth "three-and-sixes" become assimilated into British life, in fact, that many Britons coming to the United States for the first time, would spot the familiar "red-fronts" and exclaim, "Oh! Our Woolworths have come to you too!"

Birth of Today's American Woolworth

It was an April day in 1911, just a few months before C. P. Rogers made the first transcontinental airplane flight in history, that the Founder-Presidents of five Five-and-Ten syndicates met at New York's Waldorf Astoria, then on Fifth Avenue at 34th Street where the Empire State Building stands today, and considered a proposal. It was an important proposal. It proposed merger. If accepted and implemented, it would significantly affect a host of manufacturers, hundreds of landlords, thousands of employees, millions of American consumers.

The nation's population then totaled 92 million. President William Howard Taft occupied the White House. The durable Five-and-Ten was, that year, observing its 33rd Anniversary. The five merchants present were:

Seymour Horace Knox, Buffalo, New York, fifty, Founder-President of S. H. Knox & Co., then operating 108 Five-and-Tens in 14 states plus Canada. His chain was the first to cross the Canadian border.

Fred Morgan Kirby, Wilkes-Barre, Pennsylvania, fifty, Founder-President of F. M. Kirby & Co., then owning 84 "green-fronts" in 19 states. Only Kirby operated in the Deep South, and was first to penetrate the Middle West.

Charles Sumner Woolworth, Scranton, Pennsylvania, fifty-four, Founder-Proprietor of a syndicate of 14 Five-and-Tens bearing his name in Pennsylvania, New York and Maine. He was Frank Woolworth's brother, Knox's first cousin, Kirby's best friend.

Earle Perry Charlton, Fall River, Massachusetts, forty-seven, Founder-President of E. P. Charlton & Co., which operated 48 Five-and-Tens in 8 states and Canada. Charlton had introduced the Five-and-Ten to the broad region west of the Rocky Mountains.

Frank Winfield Woolworth, New York, New York, fifty-nine, Founder-President of F. W. Woolworth & Co., the field's titan and bellwether, whose "red-fronts" would number 319 by year-end, concentrated in 27 states, plus the District of Columbia, from Maine to North Carolina, from New York to Colorado.

None of the five had been born to the silk. Four of them were sons of North New York farmers, and the fifth, Charlton, was the son of a Connecticut blacksmith. The Woolworth brothers and Kirby, as seen, had apprenticed in retailing in the venerable "Corner Store" in Watertown, New York of Moore & Smith, now, in 1911, the Moore 5¢ & 10¢ Store. William Harvey Moore, seventy, their beloved mentor in youth, was the sixth, though absent that day, member of that assembled group of master merchants.

Each, at this stage of his career, also had broad outside interests. Knox, for example, was a lover of horses, and his hobby was stock farming. Among other philanthropies, he built both a Town Hall and a high school in Russell, New York, his birthplace. He was an energizer in the development of the Marine National Bank of Buffalo, an ancestor of today's Marine Midland Grace Trust Co., and for a long period served as its Chairman of the Board.

Years later, the Wilkes-Barre *Times-Leader* would profile Fred Kirby in a special Kirby Edition and would say of him, "The sun never sets on the hundreds of philanthropic projects that have felt the beneficent hand of Mr. Kirby." Also of philanthropic bent, Sum Woolworth's interests, like Kirby's, included schools, colleges, hospitals, social welfare, the gamut. Apart from funding, both of the close friends also gave of themselves. Both, for instance, were trustees of Wyoming Seminary. Kirby was a trustee, too, of Lafayette College; Woolworth served Syracuse University.

Besides his Five-and-Ten syndicate, Earle Charlton built Charlton Cotton Mills, Inc., of New England. He was also a trustee of Tufts College. During World War I he served in the War Department. He was decorated by the Republic of France.

Frank Woolworth was also a man of many parts. A lover of music, travel and the theater, he also became an avid golfer. In honor of his parents, he built and endowed the Woolworth Memorial Methodist Episcopal Church of Great Bend, New York. He served on several Boards of Directors, including the

Board of the Irving National Exchange Bank, today's Irving Trust Co. At one stage of his career, he was drafted and, for a period, served as President of the Guardian Trust Company of New York while concurrently heading his Woolworth Company.

The five were long-time friends and, in the development of their respective syndicates, were friendly in rivalry. They had always been accessible to one another for discussion and, at this Waldorf Astoria meeting, Frank Woolworth proposed that they discuss the wisdom and mutual benefit of merging the five businesses into a single national corporation. Such a corporation, by that year-end, would own and control a minimum of 590 stores in 37 states, the District of Columbia, and Canada, and command a minimum of $52 million in aggregate annual sales.

The derivable benefits from such a merger were visible and attractive. Such a consolidation would vastly expand buying power, would harness it to produce optimum purchasing and distributive economies, and would, accordingly, permit the national company to bring an even greater range of staple and luxury merchandise to consumers, coast to coast, at Five-and-Ten prices.

Merger would enable them to structure a single streamlined control and supervisory organization and a single staff of top-grade buyers. The might of a single effective organization would slash duplication; reduce waste in distribution; effect meaningful compression of operating costs; afford greater pay-as-you-go margin for store enlargement, modernization and beautification; stimulate earlier entry into more and more eligible communities and bless the new corporation with other boons.

The merchants sparred hard with Woolworth's proposal at the Waldorf that day. They weighed the "pros" and "cons" in depth. They met again and again—at the Waldorf and elsewhere. From discussion, they progressed to negotiation. From negotiation, they proceeded to structuring the proposed corporation. In the end, the five, together with William Moore, decided to merge their companies within the framework of a single national corporation.

At a meeting held at New York's Plaza Hotel on September 21, 1911, the builders of today's Woolworth, legally styled "vendors" by the merger's lawyers and "Founders" in Woolworth lore, agreed to cause the properties and assets or capital stock of their so-called "merged businesses" to be vested in a New York corporation to be formed and named F. W. Woolworth Co. The dropping of the ampersand before "Co." served to distinguish the new company from F. W. Woolworth & Co.

The agreement to consolidate was signed November 2. The new company was incorporated December 15. About it, Frank Woolworth said in his General Letter to store managers:

> Regarding store managers, the new arrangement does not affect them any more than if there were no new company to be organized, and we shall make just as few changes in store managers as heretofore.
>
> In the district offices, we have endeavored to mix the men from the various companies in all the offices so as to make the entire organization as harmonious as possible.
>
> After the first of January 1912, there will be no so-called Woolworth stores, Knox stores, Kirby stores, Charlton stores, C. S. Woolworth stores or Moore stores. It will be one harmonious whole. . . .

On March 1, 1912, F. W. Woolworth Co., today's American Woolworth, commenced operating as such, coast to coast in the United States and in the Dominion of Canada, with Frank Woolworth himself at the helm as President. S. H.

Knox, F. M. Kirby, E. P. Charlton and C. S. Woolworth were
Vice Presidents, together with Carson Peck, who was Vice
President, Treasurer and Executive Committee Chairman.
H. T. Parson was the corporation's Secretary. Mr. Moore was
named Honorary Vice President. The seven active officers composed the Executive Committee, a singularly vigorous operating instrument then to now.

As at January 1, 1912, it had this mercantile might:

| | | No. of Stores, Jan. 1, 1912 | | |
MERGED BUSINESSES	SALES FOR YEAR 1911	UNITED STATES	CANADA	TOTAL
F. W. Woolworth & Co.	$26,887,035	319	—	319
S. H. Knox & Co.	13,047,745	98	13	111
F. M. Kirby & Co.	7,253,036	96	—	96
E. P. Charlton & Co.	4,070,683	35	18	53
C. S. Woolworth	1,207,849	15	—	15
W. H. Moore	149,776	2	—	2
TOTAL	$52,616,124	565	31	596

The new corporation started life with authorized, issued
and outstanding capital stock totaling $65 million represented
by 650,000 shares of the par value of $100 each, of which
150,000 shares were 7% cumulative preferred stock, and
500,000 shares were common stock.

The $15 million cumulative preferred stock represented
tangible physical assets. The $50 million common stock
merely represented the company's good will and earning
power.[3]

[3] From its invested surplus account, American Woolworth redeemed
and retired the last of its 150,000 shares of preferred stock by February
1, 1923. From its surplus, it reduced the "good will" item in its capital
assets from $50 million in 1912 to $1 by 1925.

The corporation came into being by the simple exchange of all of its capital stock for all of the capital stock of the four merging corporations, and for all of the assets of unincorporated C. S. Woolworth and W. H. Moore.

The transaction established no public market for the stock of F. W. Woolworth Co. The six Founders, therefore, chose to offer to the public, through Goldman, Sachs & Co. and Lehman Brothers, New York, and Kleinwort Sons & Co., London, $6 million par value of $15 million of cumulative preferred stock, and $7 million par value of $50 million of common stock, apportioned among them according to their holdings.

While the Founders agreed not to dispose of any of their remaining stock for a year, they reserved the right to distribute $1.5 million par value of either preferred or common stock to the employees of the new company. The shares thus earmarked were then offered to company executives and to store managers at $50 per common share and $100 per preferred share. The stampede to buy was immediate. Treasurer Peck counseled the fortunate buyers, "Hang on to it! I say, keep it! Don't sell it any more than you would sell your birthright!"

A Board of Directors managed the company in behalf of stockholders. Comprised then of 21 members, the original F. W. Woolworth Co. Board included all seven of the active officers, a headquarters executive, the eight District Managers, three bankers, the company's General Counsel, and a retired senior S. H. Knox & Co. officer.

Not only was F. W. Woolworth Co. among the very first chain-store companies to achieve coast-to-coast stature but also was among the very first, perhaps even the first, to decentralize its administrative functions.

The 596 stores in 37 of the country's then 46 states, plus the District of Columbia and the Dominion of Canada, with which today's American Woolworth began in 1912, were grouped geographically into eight districts, each served by a fully staffed, centrally located District Office.

Headed by a responsible District Manager who was also a member of the Woolworth Board of Directors, each District Office's function, with respect to the stores within its jurisdiction, included administration, supervision, inspection, accounting, merchandising assistance, consolidation and placing of merchandise orders from the Approved List, and all other such central services.

The District Offices were located in Boston, Buffalo, Chicago, New York, San Francisco, St. Louis, Toronto and Wilkes-Barre. Intermingled here were carefully selected, functional experts from among the respective "merged businesses."

The company's statutory Principal Office became the building on the old American Corner of the public square of Watertown, New York, in which four of the six Founders received their on-the-job training in retailing. By bylaw provision, the Annual Meeting of the company's shareholders would be held there at high noon on the third Wednesday of each May.

Pending the completion of the Skyline Queen that Frank Woolworth was erecting in Manhattan's Lower City, the Stewart Building, home of American Woolworth since 1888, became the imposing Executive Office of the new corporation as well as site of its New York District Office.

In order to compensate for higher freight rates (and Canadian tariffs), the new company's fixed-price limit became 15¢ west of the Missouri River and in Canada. Elsewhere, it remained inflexibly 5¢ and 10¢.

Profit-sharing, practiced by Woolworth and the other "merged businesses" from birth, continued as the basis for executive and managerial remuneration at all Woolworth operating levels.

The requirement that all Woolworth men start at the bottom of the Woolworth ladder, the stockroom, and rise, rung by rung, on merit, remained as company policy.

The red of F. W. Woolworth & Co. was adopted as the official store-front color of F. W. Woolworth Co., and under Baron W. Gage, Construction Superintendent, all of the company's assimilated units soon became "red-fronts" uniformly except one. The Kirby "mother store" in Wilkes-Barre remained green, and continued to bear Fred Kirby's name along with its supplementary Woolworth identification.

Stores were numbered consecutively from "one" up according to their sales performance for calendar 1911, except that the huge S. H. Knox & Co. unit that was being constructed on Chicago's teeming State Street in 1911 became Store No. 1 when completed.

The Lancaster "mother" store of F. W. Woolworth & Co., the emporium that was the world's oldest Five-and-Ten, became F. W. Woolworth Co.'s Store No. 53.

The Moore store on the American Corner of Watertown's public square became Store No. 239. After 55 consecutive years on that same site, William Harvey Moore turned his keys over to F. W. Woolworth Co. on March 1, 1912. To Frank Woolworth to whom, in youth, he gave start and training, then, later, confidence and early backing, he wrote, in deep friendship:

Yesterday, I turned over to the new company, the keys that I have held for more than 55 years, with feelings of gratitude to you for the honors that you have been so instrumental in heaping upon me, and which I am unable to express in words. . . . When three score and ten years cover your head, I pray that you may be as happy as I am. . . .

CHAPTER IV

Merchant Prince's Skyqueen

Admiral Robert E. Peary reached the North Pole in 1909, and, that same year, F. W. Woolworth, as seen, introduced England to his Three-and-Six, English equivalent of his American Five-and-Ten.

Woolworth, that same eventful year, also decided to energize a second long-germinating idea, namely to erect a skyscraper permanent home for his surging company in Knickerbocker's Lower City.

As he visualized his dream structure, it would have unique stature and sheer beauty, thus enriching the architectural significance and prestige of the Empire City. By its comfort, convenience, efficiency and other advantages, furthermore, it would serve suitably as headquarters of F. W. Woolworth & Co. and home base of other prestigious tenants as well.

His dream edifice would be Gothic, like London's Houses of Parliament that he so admired. Its exterior would be a study of superb lines and tracery. Its interior would be a gem in marble. And its locale would be that site on Broadway across City Hall Park, now so tired and disheveled, that he had been studying from his window in the Stewart Building for a very long time, with mounting interest.

Woolworth Acquires Site, Taps Gilbert

At this stage the Chief owned a Woolworth Building in Lancaster that he had erected, as seen, as a monument of the birth there of his starting Five-and-Ten. Woolworth Buildings also existed that year in Trenton, New Jersey, and in Paterson, New Jersey. Having now made up his mind to proceed to build an architectural masterpiece in Gotham, he moved with typical dispatch to set his project into motion.

Assisted by his friend Lewis E. Pierson, President of the Irving National Exchange Bank, and by Edward J. Hogan, his dynamic real-estate broker, Woolworth succeeded in acquiring the corner plot on Broadway and Park Place that in New Amsterdam day had been part of the Company Farm of the Dutch West India Company. But what he had acquired was not enough to satisfy his dream. He had to have more land.

Through Hogan, he finally managed to buy the land contiguous to his Broadway and Park Place property. Totaling seven parcels measuring 152 by 197 feet in size, the large Woolworth plot now, of course, included the site of the Hone Mansion of Old New York fame during Broadway's glamor era as tree-lined Broad Way.

He next combed the country for his architect. He chose and commissioned Cass Gilbert. "This great architect was a great architect before I discovered him," Woolworth said later. "He had done great work before he touched this building. However," he added, "he is a greater architect today than he ever was."

Gilbert, who, among other architectural achievements, had designed the State Capitol of Minnesota, the New York Customs House, and the West Street Building, grasped what Woolworth had in mind, and aptly interpreted it into sketch plan.

"How high should our building be?" he had inquired. "750

feet," Woolworth had replied. "Am I limited to that?" asked Gilbert. "That's the minimum," was the answer.

Construction Feats That Skyqueen Needed

The very size of the planned skyscraper, a structure that would overtop the Pyramid of Cheops by some 300 feet, and Woolworth's and Gilbert's demand for safety at any cost, compelled special hoisting and other equipment to be devised, and amazing engineering and construction feats to be performed, in order to erect the sturdy, graceful edifice.

In order to anchor the vast skyhouse so that it would be as safe as it would be both tall and beautiful, for example, 69 huge, funnellike caissons, each some 19 feet in diameter, had to be sunk some 120 feet into solid bedrock. Filled then with concrete, these 69 solid-concrete piers supported the massive steel columns of the building.

Requiring some 24,000 tons of structural steel, and with no free storage outside of its building lines, it consequently became necessary to punch and number each gigantic steel beam in advance, and to hoist it systematically from its truck as needed.

On November 15, 1911, the rising steel of the Woolworth Building became visible above the pavement. Less than eight months later, on July 1, 1912, the American flag was unfurled at the apex of the Tower, a sixth of a mile over the sidewalks of Manhattan, heralding the completion of the steel framework.

In April 1913, the Skyline Queen was groomed and ready—set for coronation.

Charms of the Towering Queen

Like a massive cathedral of commerce attaining queendom in the mythical skyline domain of Manhattan skyscrapers, the Woolworth Building scaled 792 feet from sidewalk to crest. Towering 60 stories over the soil of New York, those 60 floors could actually have been 79 stories had the more customary "10-foot-height-per-floor" standard been chosen by the merchant and his architect. Instead, no floor of the building was less than 11 feet high and some were over 20 feet. It had a floor area totaling nearly 30 acres.

A gem of Gothic lines and tracery, the building's cream-color terra-cotta exterior was proportioned with such care and fidelity to detail that its towering height loomed trim and graceful.

Its three-story-tall entrance was an arcade of striking beauty. High over that cross-shaped main foyer, the so-called Grand Arcade, rose its vaulted dome ceiling. Studded with varicolored glass mosaic, soft yet luminous, arranged in attractive designs, the grace and richness of the dome was accentuated by soft lights concealed behind the lacelike marble cornice at the springing of the arches.

The walls themselves, tall lines rising and sweeping into graceful curves and arches, were constructed of matched marble imported from the Isle of Skyros. The cathedral-like impressiveness was carried through all of the public corridors, with floors of marble terrazzo and wainscoting of Italian marble.

Long before the modern emphasis upon natural light for building interiors, the Woolworth Building provided it. Gilbert designed the skyscraper in a U-shape, thus making every office an outside one.

Safety, besides elegance, was a hallmark of the edifice.

Constructed of enough steel to build a 10-mile-long elevated railway, and of enough bricks to pave an 11-mile-long and 30-foot-wide street, no inflammable material of any kind was used anywhere in the building's making. Reportedly, even a hurricane thrusting at 200-miles-an-hour velocity could not damage the structure's framework.

Special devices protected it even against severest lightning. Scientific studies detected no vibration anywhere in the building, including the crest of its Tower. Every stairway was an enclosed fire tower. Located in the sub-basement, a fire pump could deliver 500 gallons of water per minute to the 58th floor, against a head pressure of 820 feet.

Twenty-eight high-speed elevators not only were operated at a rate of speed unprecedented in that day but also were equipped with safety devices, including air cushions such as those first installed by Mr. Woolworth in the Woolworth Building in Lancaster. Hence, a Woolworth elevator car loaded with 7,000 pounds of material that was test-dropped from the 45th floor in free fall reached bottom without spilling a drop of the full glass of water that it carried in its test.

Each of the 28 cars, moreover, was equipped with a telephone. Connected with the central office of the Bell Telephone Company, it was possible to communicate by phone with any part of the United States from a moving elevator in the Woolworth Building.

The movement and location of each of the building's elevators, furthermore, were monitored in the Grand Arcade by an electric dispatcher system that was originated and used in this building for the first time in tall-building history.

Departmentalized, the building had its own fire, police and detective divisions, and its own cleaning, repair and general maintenance sections. Its prospective population was estimated at about 15,000, including tenants themselves and their personnel.

The first building to have its own power plant, its four huge Corliss engines were capable of generating power enough to operate an electric street railway, or to supply electric-light illumination for a city of 50,000 people.

Within a fortnight after Woolworth's sixty-first birthday, his Skyqueen was ready for crowning.

CHAPTER V

Coronation

Through newsreels, newspapers, magazines and other of that era's media of mass communication, much of New York had followed the evolution of the Woolworth Building from a massive hole deep in the bowels of Manhattan to a towering colossus of steel.

Yet the multitudes of the Empire City, and of its environs within vision range, who were to witness the first illumination of Knickerbocker's Skyline Queen that spring evening of her crowning, were probably unprepared for the full dazzling impact of that first sight.

Inside the building itself, the 27th floor had been converted into an imposing banquet hall. There, that evening, April 24, 1913, some 800 guests of Frank Woolworth had gathered both to dedicate the edifice and to join him in honoring Cass Gilbert, its architect.[4]

[4] The hard-cover, privately published (1913) book, *The Dinner Given to Cass Gilbert by F. W. Woolworth* (New York Public Library, Class Mark IRH), not only publishes all of the dinner speeches in full but also embodies the complete attendance list and the table-seating list.

A distinguished assembly, its number included the Secretary of the Treasury; the Lieutenant Governors of Massachusetts, New York and Rhode Island; a former Governor of New York; foreign diplomats and dignitaries; mayors, and over a hundred U.S. Senators and U.S. Representatives, serving 28 states, who had journeyed from Washington to Manhattan on the "Woolworth Special" dispatched for Woolworth by the Pennsylvania Railroad.

The assembly included William Gibbs McAdoo, Charles M. Schwab, Elbert H. Gary, for example, and other prominent industrialists, bankers, jurists, publishers, educators, scientists, surgeons, authors and artists. Another "Woolworth Special" had brought the host's New England guests.

It included, of course, Woolworth's relatives and his closest friends and associates—C. S. Woolworth, W. H. Moore, Carson Peck, Fred Kirby, Seymour Knox—the full list. It included Woolworth men who, since youth, had helped to develop the Woolworth Five-and-Ten; sources of supply who, through the years, had grown with the Woolworth syndicate; others whose association with the host was long and mutually prized.

Behold Her Skyline Majesty!

When all were seated, the lights were extinguished. Outside, only the bare outline of the unlit building was discernible in the darkness of that spring evening. Concurrently, the ready signal was flashed to President Woodrow Wilson in the White House. He responded by pressing a button connected by wire with the Skyline Queen in distant Manhattan. His act was timed at exactly 7:30 P.M.

Immediately and for the first time, 80,000 electric lights, enough to illuminate the entire 40-mile waterfront of Manhattan Island, were ablaze in the skyscraper, from summit to ground.

In the banquet room, cued to that flash, the orchestra struck up the national anthem.

Outside, over a radius of miles, waiting multitudes thrilled to the sight as the beautiful colossus, bathed abruptly in millions of candlepower of light, sprang radiant into view like a shaft of glistening alabaster against the blackness of that spring Thursday night.

Assembly Hears Merchant Prince

F. Hopkinson Smith, distinguished author and painter, was the banquet's toastmaster. He called first upon Louis J. Horowitz, President of Thompson-Starrett Co., builder; then upon William Winter, critic, poet and man of letters; then upon W. U. Hensel, Attorney General of the Commonwealth of Pennsylvania, cradle of the Woolworth Five-and-Ten. His guests then heard from Frank Woolworth, host.

After extolling Cass Gilbert and those others who actually built the Woolworth Building, the Chief warmly recognized men, near and dear to him, who indirectly had made the structure possible.

"On March 24, 1873, over forty years ago," he said, "I went to work to learn the dry goods business in Watertown, New York with Moore and Smith. I am very thankful to my employers. They taught me the first lessons in my mercantile career. . . . They are here tonight, and I want you all to know them. Mr. Moore and Mr. Smith, stand up, please."

When the applause for the veteran merchants had stilled, Mr. Woolworth next presented his brother, Charles Sumner Woolworth, "the first manager," he said, "that I selected after I had run the first store successfully." He then focused attention upon the tables seating Carson Peck, Clinton Case, Harry Moody, Hubert Parson, Alvin Ivie, and other Woolworth stalwarts who, he said, "helped me to collect the nickels and dimes that have made this building possible."

He welcomed Lewis J. Pierson, banker, and Edward J. Hogan, real-estate broker, who had helped him land the Woolworth site. Then, he directed the assembly's attention to the many manufacturers who had, in effect, matured in the service of the Diamond W, saying: "Seated at the tables right there in front of me are gentlemen from whom I have made a great many purchases in years gone by, and it is a great pleasure for me to greet these gentlemen here tonight. . . ."

He announced that, by actual measurement, the average height of the Tower was 792 feet, 1 inch. Above sea level, high tide, the Tower was 947 feet, 2 inches.

"One fine day," he added, "I went to the very pinnacle of the Tower, and walked down from that exalted height to the sub-basement of the building. . . . The building as it stands is 60 stories high."

Unplanned Statuettes That Grace Arcade

"For most men," Cass Gilbert said in his address that followed Woolworth's, "the financing alone would have been a staggering proposition. For him," he added, "it was easy. He just cut it out. His banker told me that this structure is unique in New York, and perhaps in the whole history of great buildings in this country, in that it stands here tonight without a mortgage and without a single dollar indebtedness."

Naming names, Gilbert then lauded the efforts of the corps of craftsmen, each a standout in his field and each present, who composed his team that built the Woolworth Building.

Thomas Johnson, of Gilbert's staff, by the way, had had

grotesque statuettes of Woolworth, Gilbert, Pierson and Horowitz sculptured without either the Chief's or Gilbert's knowledge, and had had them fitted into near-ceiling niches in the
Grand Arcade. Woolworth's posed him counting out nickels
and dimes; Gilbert's had him holding the building in his arms.
The others were equally apt. Frank Woolworth, on sight, was
simply delighted with them, gleefully ordered that they forever
stand in place. They have interested Grand Arcade traffic ever
since.

When Gilbert resumed his seat, Woolworth rose, and, from
somewhere, a gigantic silver cup embellished with an engrav-
ing of the building, obviously the product of master hands,
appeared on the dais. "Now, Mr. Gilbert," he said, "You
thought that you were through but, unfortunately, you have to
get back on your hind legs.

"It has been said that some architects never associate with
their clients after they put up one building for them. It has
been said that the client never cared to see the architect again.
Mr. Gilbert is just as much my friend today as he ever was.[5]
Therefore, I give him this little token of my regard."

Empire Room

The Woolworth Building was created at a cold-cash cost to
Mr. Woolworth of $13.5 million expended through the Broad-
way Park Place Company that he formed, owned, and headed
to his death. It was managed by it to 1924, when the building
was sold to F. W. Woolworth Co.'s Woolco Realty Corporation.

Having rented the entire 24th floor to house its Executive

[5] Three years later, Cass Gilbert created Woolworth's Winfield Hall in
Glen Cove, New York.

Office, and the south wing of the 23rd floor to quarter its New York District Office, F. W. Woolworth Co. moved into its imposing new headquarters, late in April 1913, from its quarter-century home in the Stewart Building just across City Hall Park.

For his own private office, and to serve his presidential successors in years ahead, Woolworth selected a suite on the 24th floor, 30 feet square, facing south and east. Years before, he had been fascinated by the beauty of the Empire Room of Napoleon's palace in Compiègne, France. Now he decided to have an Empire Room, as nearly like the original as possible, for himself now, for his successors later.

He commissioned antique and art dealers of Paris and New York to carry out his plans. In his February 20, 1914, General Letter, he evaluated the result as fulfilling his wish for beauty plus efficiency.

The room's cream-and-gold coloring included a cream-white ceiling embossed with gold decorations. Wall panels and wainscoting were of Vert Campan marble from the north of Italy, with pilasters of dark marble and Empire capitals covered with gold. There was a 24-inch marble floor border around the room. Each door had eight panels with bronze mountings made in Paris of mercury gilt. Each panel had its own distinctive bronze-and-gold mounted figure.

The mantel of the large fireplace was made of green Tyros marble, with mercury gilt bronze ornaments. Over it was a ceiling-high mirror. And on the west wall hung the large oil portrait of Napoleon in coronation robes that had been faithfully copied for Mr. Woolworth from the original at Versailles. After the Chief's death, by the way, the company replaced the Napoleon with a handsome equal-size oil portrait of Frank Woolworth, as a mark of its esteem.

The Empire-design desk was made of solid mahogany, with gilt bronze mountings and a green leather top with hand-

tooled gilt edge. Inkwell, paperweight and other desk accouterments were bronze and Napoleonic.

Carved and finished in old gold, and upholstered in red,
pink and gold handmade tapestry, the chairs were faithful
replicas of the famous Throne Chair in the Palace of Fontainebleau.

Mr. Woolworth considered the clock on the fireplace
mantel a crowning feature of the Empire Room. Carved in
gold to the likeness of Cleopatra, the clockpiece had been
purchased by him in Paris in late 1913, and is said to have
been presented to Napoleon Bonaparte, over a century before,
by the Czar of Russia.

Home Front's Empire Room Ally

From the Empire Room, Frank Woolworth presided over
booming Woolworth for nearly six years after his Skyqueen's
dedication, five during the ordeal of World War I and its
consequences on the home front.

The assassination of Austrian Grand Duke Ferdinand in
Sarajevo, Serbia, having finally impelled Europe into long-
hovering war in 1914, the overriding stress of combatants,
then and thereafter, was upon generating war might so as to
win peace. The production power of nations became concentrated upon that vital goal.

Although the United States did not at first enter the conflict,
its production capacity was taxed to the limit to help feed,
clothe, arm the embattled world. Under such stress, many new
production processes were perfected. Volume of fabricated
goods swelled. Many factories switched to making munitions
and other war materiel. Entrance into war in 1917 accelerated
the nation's previous peak production pace. America's prime
focus, and that of her allies, was upon winning the war and

restoring peace. To a large extent, therefore, domestic distribution was left to adjust itself to the country's emergency conditions as best it could.

Shortages of needed material and outright lack of some; loss of manpower to the armed forces or to war plants and shipyards; transportation delays and obstructions; conversion of many civilian goods producers to the making of war apparatus—these and other causes contributed toward slashing the output of merchandise for domestic consumption even as imports diminished to a trickle.

Consumers shouted for goods that were soon in short supply. Effects of war forced manufacturers' costs sky-high, and their consequent prices commensurately higher. Civilian merchandise, therefore, was not only scarce but also expensive.

One by one, other Five-and-Ten companies took on higher-price lines simply because they could not buy enough merchandise to sell profitably for nickels and dimes. Woolworth was the single exception. The merchant in the Empire Room steadfastly refused to budge from the fixed price limits of American Woolworth. And the flexibility and expertise of the Woolworth organization, the skill of its master buyers, the strength of its manufacturer relations, and the buying and selling might of the network buttressed the Empire Room.

Woolworth had already standardized its leading lines of merchandise. Its buying experts now concentrated not only upon ferreting out substitutes for goods gone to war but also, as production consultants, upon helping American manufacturers to fabricate goods profitably that had exclusively been imported before World War I. Woolworth's guarantee against loss, and the extent of its volume buying, were persuasive inducements.

Christmas tree decorations, as one example, were then solely made in Germany, as seen. When Mars over Europe halted their export, Woolworth turned to America's production wizardry for action to satisfy the demand of the nation's Home Front for ornaments to brighten the yuletide. American production experiments were backed by Woolworth, and its buyers, world's largest purchasers of such goods, were invaluable in their help. The experiments were successful. Guaranteed against loss by Woolworth, the manufacturer then launched mass production. In due time, American-made ornaments were streaming from the production line to Woolworth stores for sale at Woolworth prices. A new American industry was thus born.

Stocked with a vast range of values throughout that war period, Woolworth "red-fronts" met consumer demand head-on. In a single war year of shortages and soaring prices, for instance, Woolworth sold to its customers, at nickel and dime prices; over 20 million toys; 15 million cakes of soap; 350,000 barrels of glassware; 5 million papers of hairpins; 9 million yards of curtain material; 3 million boxes of crochet and embroidery cotton; 20 million pieces of enamelware; 100 million picture postcards—naming only a few among its host of large-volume sales.

Under the firm hand in the Empire Room, American Woolworth made a record passage through the turbulence of World War I. Compared with 1913, when its 683 "red-fronts" produced over $66 million in sales, Woolworth's 1,039 Five-and-Tens achieved sales aggregating over $107 million in 1918. A billion people were estimated to have entered and browsed in Woolworth stores in the United States and Canada in 1918. Over 824 million were estimated to have purchased goods while there.

Then, on April 2, 1919, Frank Woolworth departed the Woolworth business that he had shaped, and the Woolworth Building that he had erected, for the very last time. And neither they nor the Empire Room saw him thereafter.

CHAPTER VI

Sixty Years After

Some six decades, four American wars, and a more than doubling of the nation's population after the Woolworth Building's dedication, Frank Woolworth's skyqueen and F. W. Woolworth Co. itself are hale, current and competitive. Structured for durability, both have coped well with the vicissitudes of those sixty eventful years.

During the first decade following the Woolworth Building's debut, American Woolworth made steady, even spectacular, further progress as the purchasing agent of the consumer, but it was also assaulted by death. In a single fifteen-month span between April 1915 and May 1916 it lost two of its Founders, namely Seymour Horace Knox and William Harvey Moore; its great administrator, Carson C. Peck; and a rising star, Charles C. Griswold.

Expiring in April 1915, Carson Peck, fifty-seven, was first to pass. A grieving Frank Woolworth articulated his sorrow in a General Letter obituary. "I have known Mr. Peck better than any other man living," he said. "I have been with him day-by-day, week-by-week, month-by-month, for nearly 27 years." He extolled him as a man, merchant, associate, friend.

Member of a family whose roots in Jefferson County dated from earliest New York Colonial era, Peck was buried on a hill in Watertown. The Carson C. Peck Memorial Hospital, erected by his wife and family, stands in his memory in his loved Brooklyn, the community into which he had moved in 1890 and of which, as resident and newspaper owner, he had become a prominent part.

Some 17 days after Peck's death, Seymour Knox, fifty-four, died in Buffalo. Reeling from this second great blow, the Chief mourned the loss of his favorite cousin, his close friend from boyhood. He ordered every Woolworth store to close on the day of Knox's funeral, just as he had done for Peck. "The above," he said in concluding his impressive Knox obituary, "is only a brief outline of Mr. Knox's fruitful business career. If someone could write his biography in full, it would be a mighty good lesson for any young man to read."

A year to the very day after Knox's passing, William Moore, seventy-five, was preparing in Watertown for the arrival of Frank Woolworth from the West Coast to preside at the Annual Meeting of American Woolworth to be held at high noon of the following day, May 17, 1916. He had planned to meet his friend's train. He had planned an elaborate luncheon to occur during his Watertown stay. Instead, he kept an unplanned engagement—a date with death. He expired suddenly that late afternoon while reading his evening paper in his usual chair in his living room.

On a table at his side when he succumbed stood the large Circassian walnut humidor that had been presented to him nearly a decade ago, at a sumptuous testimonial banquet honoring his sixty-fifth birthday and his fiftieth anniversary in business on the American Corner, tendered to him in Watertown by the family of Woolworth executives, buyers and managers. On the silver top of that square container, first of its kind and specially designed for him by master hands, were

inset 50 nickels and 50 dimes, and they bordered the signatures of the Woolworth brothers, Knox, Kirby and 180 Woolworth men and women.

Hardly had the mortal remains of his respected great friend
been interred in Watertown than Frank Woolworth set into
motion the erection of a six-story building on the site of the
old Corner Store in that community, to serve not only as
a memorial to William Harvey Moore but also as the statutory
Principal Office of American Woolworth. But World War I
and after-war conditions delayed its completion. It was
opened in July 1921.

Passing of the Chief

Some five months after Marshal Ferdinand Foch, in a railroad
coach in Compiègne Forest, France, signed the Armistice
victoriously terminating World War I, Frank Woolworth was
at his office and, to his satisfaction, received a glowing report
of burgeoning Woolworth sales from Hubert Parson, then
Vice President, Treasurer and General Manager. Feeling un-
well that day, April 2, 1919, he then left for home—unknow-
ingly for the last time.

He worked with his secretary at his town house the next
day, then, on Friday, left for the country for the weekend. By
the time that he reached Winfield Hall, his sore throat had
worsened and he was suffering recurring chills. His pains and
high fever increased. His doctors battled a combination of
uremic and septic poisoning, gallstones, and a throat infection,
in vain. He expired at 1:50 A.M. on April 8, 1919, exactly five
days short of his sixty-seventh birthday.

Newspapers, here and abroad, widely reported his death,
profiled his life, evaluated his deeds. The New York *Sun*'s
appraisal was internationally picked up. "He won a fortune,"

it said, "not in showing how little could be sold for much but how much could be sold for little."

The simple but stirring funeral service was held in the music room of the Woolworth town house in the forenoon of April 10, 1919. It was conducted by Bishop John William Hamilton of the Methodist Episcopal Church, the Reverend Dr. S. Parkes Cadman, and Reverend Smith W. Brown, formerly of Watertown.

Long-time friends and associates came from close and far to pay their last respects: men who, side by side with him, had helped to blaze the trail of the Five-and-Ten; men who had followed him as young men and who had retired wealthy and honored; producers who, years before, had shared his vision and whose enterprises grew as Woolworth grew; men in other fields who were near to him in life and mourned him in death.

The Executive Office, all District Offices, all Woolworth stores in the United States, Canada, England, Scotland, Ireland and Wales were closed at least on the day of the funeral. In the Woolworth Building, every elevator, every activity controlled by the building, was halted while the funeral rites of the skyscraper's sire were in progress.

One of the most touching acts of esteem stemmed from Detroit, site of the Executive Office of S. S. Kresge Co. During the hour of Frank Woolworth's funeral, every Kresge Five-and-Ten was closed by order of Sebastian S. Kresge himself.

The remains of the Chief were laid to rest in a mausoleum in Woodlawn Cemetery. And with his passing phased the foundation stage of Woolworth, the company.

At a meeting that June, the Board of Directors adopted a resolution memorializing its deceased leader and ordered that it be spread upon the minutes of that meeting to pass into posterity as the sense of the corporation and all of its elements. As a further mark of respect and esteem, it acted to keep the seat of F. W. Woolworth on that Board vacant for a full year.

Another Woolworth, Charles Sumner Woolworth, sixty-two, was elevated to the newly created position of Chairman of the Board. And to the presidency itself the Board elected Hubert Templeton Parson, forty-seven, veteran of 27 years of grooming and performance under the eye of the Chief himself. He thus became the first man other than the Chief ever to head the company bearing the F. W. Woolworth name.

Surging Woolworth Passes 50th Anniversary

Ten years later, F. W. Woolworth Co., under Hubert Parson, observed its 50th Anniversary internationally.

"A man can reach fifty years of age," said Parson during that Golden Anniversary, "without doing anything of consequence. But a company could not achieve fifty years of life unless it was motivated by sound principles, generated forward by effective operation, and continuously satisfied the public interest. We have aggressively pursued the teachings of our founder and, by performance, have, therefore, attained fifty years of public service."

By that year-end 1929, American Woolworth either owned or controlled 2,247 "red-fronts" in the United States, Canada, Cuba, England, Scotland, Ireland, Wales and Germany.

The Diamond W had entered Cuba in 1924. And in 1926, posthumously fulfilling another idea of Frank Woolworth, the parent company had launched F. W. Woolworth Co., G.m.b.H. in Germany through German-speaking American Woolworth "Volunteer-Pioneers" led by Richard H. Strongman. The American-controlled German company had opened the first Woolworth "25 und 50 pfg. laden" in Bremen in July 1927. So instantly successful had been that "mother" store that it had been joined by eight other thriving Woolworth units, operating in other cities of the Republic of Germany, by that 1927 year-end.

In 1929, American Woolworth also controlled French

Woolworth, which performed assembling and other such functions in Paris and Calais but operated no stores in France. It also owned an agency for assembling and warehousing in Sonneberg, Germany. Its three American and Canadian warehouses were located in New York, San Francisco and Toronto.

Compared with $119 million in American and Canadian sales in 1919, death year of the Chief, F. W. Woolworth Co. had American, Canadian and Cuban sales at the end of its Golden Jubilee Year in 1929 aggregating $303 million.

That same year, when the United States meant a nation of 122 million people, with $83 billion in national income and $49 billion in retail sales, it was estimated that approximately 90 million persons a week entered the nation's motion-picture houses coast to coast. By comparison, it was estimated that some 60 million Americans weekly entered and browsed in Woolworth stores that same year.

Accelerates to Its Diamond Anniversary

The nation turned the 1920's and landed smack into its history's most drastic economic depression. In the march of time, step by step, then came the New Deal, including its experiment in industrial self-government that helped to restore confidence; economic recovery; the National Defense Program; Pearl Harbor, World War II, and America as the Arsenal of Democracy; victory and reconversion from wartime to peacetime economy; affluence, deeper incursion into the Atomic Age, and incredible scientific developments. In 1954, F. W. Woolworth Co. observed its Diamond Anniversary.

In orderly succession, four men respectively held the presidency of Woolworth during the 1929–1954 quarter-century.

Hubert Parson, the Chief's successor, reached retirement

age in 1932. He gave way that year to Byron DeWitt Miller, fifty-seven, who, in turn, was succeeded by Charles Wurtz Deyo, fifty-six, in 1936.

In 1944, C. S. Woolworth, eighty-seven, stepped down from the office of Chairman of the Board that he had occupied since his brother's passing in 1919, and was acclaimed and voted the company's Honorary Chairman.[6] Mr. Deyo succeeded Mr. Woolworth as Board Chairman, and continued as President.

Two years later, the position of Chairman of the Board was made an active office, and Mr. Deyo retained it. He was succeeded as President by Alfred Lester Cornwell, sixty-two. When Charles Deyo retired in 1950, Mr. Cornwell was elected Chairman while concurrently holding the presidency. Mr. Deyo was Honorary Chairman to his death in 1952.

Each of the four—Parson, Miller, Deyo, Cornwell—had several decades of Woolworth experience, bottom to top, before rising to the Woolworth helm.

Picking up the reins from Hubert Parson as the nation's economy continued to plummet, Byron Miller piloted Woolworth through the Great Depression. The company that had never before taken a step backward, and never again since, had had sales declines in 1930–1932, as did practically every other company during that period of practically motionless business. Its annual net income never totaled less than the $22 million for 1932, however, and the Woolworth dividend, paid as regularly as clockwork before and since, was paid as usual throughout that critical economic depression.

[6] Helena Woolworth McCann, Frank Woolworth's oldest daughter, was elected to his seat on the Woolworth Board of Directors in 1920 and served to her death in 1938. Jessie Woolworth Donahue, his youngest daughter, was also elected in 1920, and served to 1944. Edna Woolworth Hutton, second daughter, predeceased her father. She died in 1917.

It was during Byron Miller's administration that the hallowed Woolworth10¢ fixed price limit was relaxed. Advocated by Charles Deyo, then Vice President overseeing buying, a 20¢ price line was adopted in 1932, in the nadir of depression. The move was made so as to enable Woolworth's vast purchasing power to evacuate spectacular merchandise values from the fallen markets (the Chief would have called them "plums" and "corkers"), and bring them to the country's tight-budgeted consumers at fixed 20¢ prices at a time when every penny had to do extra duty. By the close of President Miller's administration the company's sales were again on the upsweep.

Under President Deyo, who led Woolworth through World War II, its "red-fronts" became variety stores, thus demonstrating the company's ingrained flexibility. Championed by its new leader, the present policy of offering a wide range of merchandise without respect to arbitrary maximum prices was adopted, thus keeping Woolworth abreast of, and competitive in, the fast-changing patterns of the retail marketplace. During the Deyo presidency, sales escalated from $290 million in 1936 to $477 million in 1945.

The tenure of Alfred Cornwell, President during the post–World War II period, was marked by the greatest sales boom in Woolworth history to 1954, the company's Diamond Anniversary. Volume burgeoned from $477 million in 1945 to over $700 million in 1954. During that span, moreover, the company's outlay for store modernization and improvement alone aggregated over $175 million.

Earle Perry Charlton, sixty-seven, was the first of the last three of the Founders who expired during that 1929–1954 quarter-century. He died in 1930, thereby leaving only Sum Woolworth and Fred Kirby as survivors. The two maintained a close, 60-year-old friendship that had started in boyhood at Moore & Smith.

Though Woolworth's Scranton and Kirby's Wilkes-Barre "mother" stores had long since been absorbed by F. W. Woolworth Co. (Kirby's still wore his name), both much-honored philanthropists continued to watch over them like barnyard roosters. Each lost no opportunity to crow mirthfully when his old store, on occasion, happened to outperform the other. In one such instance, this speeded from Founder Sum to Founder Fred:

> A month or so ago, when I had a slight attack of stomach trouble and was feeling rather badly in consequence, I received a letter from you in which you appeared to be quite distressed over the fact that the Scranton store was not showing up favorably as compared with the Wilkes-Barre store in regard to sales and cost-to-sell.
>
> Whether you wrote that letter in order to make me feel badly, thinking to take advantage of my weak condition, or whether you wanted me to straighten it out myself, is problematical. However, I call your attention to the report received this very morning in which Scranton shows sales exceeding those of Wilkes-Barre, and at a sales cost of almost $1 less per $100. . . .

Fred Kirby predeceased Sum Woolworth by nearly seven years. In October 1940, at seventy-eight, he succumbed to pneumonia at his Glen Summit, Pennsylvania, home and was buried with honors in Wilkes-Barre, the loving community that for years had demonstrated its respect and esteem for him on the annual "Kirby Day" that it had initiated.[7]

In 1947, Woolworth suffered the loss of its last Woolworth, its last Founder. C. S. Woolworth, ninety, expired at his

---

[7] The book, *The Christmas Caravan of Love,* by Hugh Weir, was published as a Christmas tribute to Kirby in 1927. It embodies facsimiles of the personal letters of esteem written, on that occasion, by 83 of his closest friends.

Scranton home in January, and was buried in that Pennsylvania community which for years had showered him with affection. As with Kirby, the grieving company's directors, executives, key personnel, those who knew him in life and mourned him in death, came to the Scranton funeral to pay their last respects. The company honored the memory of a pioneer, the last of its Founding Fathers.

$700 Million Annual Sales and Escalating

Back in 1907, in the era of the horsecar when Woolworth meant 160 "red-fronts," the Chief pored over his sales figures and wrote in his General Letter:

> The business as a whole has been phenomenal, and the total sales for the year reached $15 million—an unheard of figure, and an unthinkable figure, five years ago. . . . How long this can keep up only the future can tell. We have never taken a step backward, and trust we never will. . . . This work will go on and on after all of us are dead and gone. . . .

By its Diamond Anniversary in 1954, F. W. Woolworth Co., as seen, had already passed the $700 million annual sales mark and was climbing steadily. Aside from well over 2,000 "Woolworths" in the United States, Canada and Cuba, it not only controlled British Woolworth, which operated 800 stores in England, Scotland, Eire and Wales, but also German Woolworth, which had made noteworthy postwar recovery and was operating 50 thriving units in West Germany at 1954 year-end.

Unlike many other business giants, Woolworth owned no mines or natural resources, no factories, and only the irreducible minimum of real-estate properties that might come under the designation of "plant."

Its greatest single asset, transcendent asset from birth through 75 years of Woolworth, was still people.

Interpreting and satisfying the will and whim of people as consumers was still Woolworth's prime mercantile function, and its effectiveness in performing that function had justified its existence through the years, and had generated its decade-by-decade growth to its Diamond Anniversary status.

Woolworth recognized very early in his career that the customer is not always the consumer, and that when one member of the household buys for another, it is the ultimate consumer, not alone the customer, who must be satisfied. He therefore inaugurated then the privilege of "return" or "refund" for his customers. It was still basic policy as the company observed its 75th Anniversary. It stands as firmly today.

By the very nature of their function, Woolworth stores had to be involved in, and closely identified with, the communities and neighborhoods in which located. Hence it is no coincidence that many an illustrator, when he set out to background a Main Street scene in 1954, as before, used a Woolworth store as backdrop. Scarcely an adult, when he recalled his home-town younger days, did not fondly recollect some excursions into the exciting emporium with the Diamond W and the red-and-gold Woolworth sign across its façade. And, wherever he now lived, chances were that Woolworth was still his neighbor.

Woolworth never has had an average or typical customer. Every person who ever entered a "Woolworth" has been an individual with his own tastes and preferences, free to pick and choose, to reject or purchase. As Frank Woolworth had persistently emphasized, therefore, every Woolworth manager in 1954, as before, had to be on constant reconnaissance to determine consumer demand in his own store and to satisfy such demand. Furthermore, as an important merchant and respected member of the community, he was encouraged and expected by his company to participate in civic affairs.

He had the responsibility of sharing in the support of worthy local welfare enterprises, and had a budget from which to make worthy contributions and donations. He was accountable to his company for the kind of reputation that it enjoyed in the community. He was the key not only of Woolworth's present there but also of its future.

From earliest Woolworth day, the store itself has been the first rung up the Woolworth ladder to store management and beyond. From the ranks of its so-called "Learners" eventually came its ace store managers who, in authority commensurate with responsibility, were equivalent to owners of individually owned establishments of substantial stature and significance.

From store-management ranks, in turn, came its District Managers (now Regional Vice Presidents) who were, in effect, equivalent to heads of large-volume regional chain-store companies; came its District Office (now Regional Office) executives and specialists; eventually came its Executive Office operating and functional executives; ultimately came the hands at its very helm, namely its Presidents and its Board Chairmen.

Though Frank Woolworth was the energizer of the Woolworth "Learner" recruitment and training program from scratch, efficient, compassionate Carson Peck, his second in command and program administrator, was closer to the "Learner," monitored his progress and was, in fact, known throughout the syndicate as the "Learner's" patron saint.

In that day when necessary store expansion was largely predicated upon how fast handpicked neophytes could be recruited, trained and developed into effective assistant store managers, then small-store managers, then larger-store managers, their in-depth training and indoctrination were largely on the job by exacting store managers who regularly reported on them to Peck. Duration mainly depended upon their readiness for deserved promotion when the right store opportunities materialized.

In 1954, its Diamond Anniversary, Woolworth's modern, structured "Learners" training program, geared to develop trained merchants ready for store management, spanned from 36 to 48 months, depending upon circumstances and the individual. Each of the chosen received a good starting salary, regular increases commensurate with earned progress, and wide-open chance someday to occupy an office in the Cathedral of Commerce. Today, the program includes women, as would be expected of a company that, as seen, had female store managers from as far back in its history as the able Mary Ann Creighton and Mrs. A. C. Coons, dynamic "Lady of Syracuse." During World War II, for instance, women managed over 500 Woolworth units; many others filled other important posts.

As it observed its 75th Anniversary, Woolworth's family of people included 88,000 stockholders; 93,000 employees in the United States, Canada and Cuba alone; thousands of manufacturers and other sources of supply, and a quantity of customers of all ages and kinds that was so large and repetitive as to be impossible of reliable estimate.

Generation after generation of these consumers had come to regard the name "Woolworth" as synonymous with the term "Five-and-Ten" as a distinctive store type. Woolworth's faithful consumer millions went to what many still considered "Five-and-Tens" to browse and buy in 1954, even though the incredible values that they purchased in Woolworth were priced economically but no longer within fixed nickel-and-dime limits.

The public, during the Diamond Anniversary, did not yet think of Woolworth as one of the nation's largest purveyors of food service. Nonetheless, the company already operated a thousand in-store restaurants, luncheonettes, snack bars, soda fountains and bake shops, and was already one of the country's largest buyers of farm products.

In a single year, for instance, it bought from farmers, in quantity, for cash, 4 million pounds of beef; 1.5 million pounds of ham; 4 million pounds of poultry; 3 million pounds of fresh and frozen eggs; 15 million pounds of potatoes; 5 million pounds of flour, etc. Its vast purchase of turkeys, as a further example, succeeded in transforming that bird from a holiday feature brightening Thanksgiving, Christmas and other family festive occasions and the groaning boards of banquets to a staple dish on Woolworth's daily menus at Woolworth prices.

Backdrop of Woolworth Operation 1954–1972

The face and figure and, to a meaningful extent, the mind and spirit of the United States changed substantially as it added girth and maturing years during the period between 1954, the year of Woolworth's Diamond Anniversary, and 1972.

Within that 18-year period, four Presidents had successively occupied the White House, namely Presidents Eisenhower, Kennedy, Johnson and Nixon—two Democrats sandwiched between two Republicans. Population had skyrocketed from 150 million to over 200 million. Migration from hinterland had saturated both the East Coast and the West Coast. Suburbia had flowered everywhere. Plants and factories had industrialized much of rural America. Many cities had swelled to overflowing proportions, and most of these were battling grave internal social and economic problems. Meantime, in approximately the same period, gross national product had soared from $285 billion to over $1 trillion and was still ascending.

Modern, jet-fast aircraft had further shortened America's domestic and international distances of travel, and an unprecedented travel boom had developed as commercial aviation expanded the safety, comfort and convenience of air travel, and priced cost to the pocketbook of more and more people. Products of science prototyped and pioneered in the past had become the developed and perfected actualities of the present: air conditioning, Bakelite, the electron tube, the gyrocompass, the cyclotron, the electronic computer, polio vaccine, radar, the rocket motor, uranium fission, cortisone, neoprene, sulfanilamide, the transistor, so many others.

Milestone events had abounded during the period, including, for random example, the conquering of Mount Everest; the launching of *Nautilus,* the U.S.'s first atomic submarine; the wedding of Big Labor by the merging of AFL and CIO; the first transatlantic jet airline service; the opening of the St. Lawrence Seaway; USSR's Sputnik I; demonstrated attainment of nuclear competency by Great Britain, France and Communist China, in that order, after the U.S.A. and U.S.S.R.; and, undoubtedly the premier among a host of other prime mileposts, namely the three-times landing and on-the-spot exploration of the moon itself by American astronauts.

The swelling American nation, hurting with growing pains and grappling with the urgency that its people learn to live harmoniously together and with the changes and effects of great growth, had come face to face with social upheaval. Influencing issues, randomly listed, included civil rights, morality, student and other dissent, civil disobedience, social welfare, drugs, racism and a long list of other headings, including substantial antagonism to the Vietnam War expressed by many demonstrations and some pitched battles.

There was hue and cry for corrective action to subdue pollution of the nation's air and waterways; for effective quelling of the growing wave of crime and violence, especially in the cities; for a more successful war against poverty in a country so rich; for really meaningful action against inflation and the causes producing upward spiraling of prices; for more and better housing, improved transportation, higher quality schools for all children irrespective of race, creed, color; for slashing unemployment; stabilization of rents; lower taxes; a better deal for the nation's millions of senior citizens; for a gamut of other advocated boons over banes.

America surely had shortcomings in 1972, just as every other nation had them. But its taken-for-granted strengths, as always, far exceeded its weaknesses. And its 1946–1971 period had been an era of unmatched progress.

In that latest available span, population rose from 142 million to over 207 million, and presaged a population of about 300 million by the year 2000. Moreover, that 46 percent population explosion had been accompanied by a rise in 1946–1971 production of 138 percent.

Americans in 1971 were better fed, had better incomes, lived in better homes, better equipped with household appliances, than even a generation ago, when their standard of living was recognized as world's highest. Length of life averaged four years longer due to advances of medical science. Average weekly wage in manufacturing, as an example, had been $43.32 in 1946—was $143.64 in 1971. Personal per capita income before taxes had been $1,264 in 1946—in 1971 was $4,178, meaning a $2,914 rise. Prices, to be sure, had gone up with earnings.

In that era of development unparalleled anywhere in the world, the number of employed individuals had mounted from 55 million to 80 million. Whereas about 50 percent of the nation's families had owned an automobile in 1946, about 80 percent had at least one car in 1971. And with the wider spread of the nation's wealth had also come increased saving. Total value of savings-bank accounts jumped from $59 billion in 1946 to $448 billion in 1971.

Despite this glowing record, however, the nation still had much to do. Foremost, it had to uplift its disadvantaged to a higher standard of living. There was mounting public demand for constructive action to that end.

The country's total production output in 1946 at 1971 prices was reportedly $445 billion. In the third quarter of 1971, total output was reportedly running at $1,059 billion, meaning a 138 percent gain in 25 years.

Much of those vast production aggregates was for consumer goods that mass producers depended upon mass distributors to bring effectively to the nation's consumers in the retail marketplace. That marketplace changed substantially in the 1946–1971 period.

Back in 1946, large-scale retailers were principally of two basic types—"vertical" and "horizontal."

The so-called "vertical" distributors were primarily large department stores whose departmentalized sales outlets—clothing, furniture, toy, haberdashery, the gamut—were concentrated under one roof. Though some had a branch or two, and some even had affiliation with other department stores, generally each was autonomous, self-sufficient, and achieved its year's large sales volume wholly in that single, departmentalized emporium.

The "horizontal" mass distributors were the multi-unit retail corporations such as Woolworth, A & P, Sears Roebuck, Penney, Walgreen, etc., whose sales performance was accomplished through a number of uniformly identified, widely scattered stores operating under common management, ownership or ultimate capital control, and engaged in the sale of the same general kind of goods, wares and merchandise.

Better known as "chain stores," these corporations were national or sectional or local in operating scope. Though the Census Bureau listed 86 different types of chain stores, six types were generally considered the very backbone of chain stores in America, namely general merchandise (including variety store), food, apparel, shoe, drug and restaurant.

After World War II and the reconversion to peacetime economy, the field of retail distribution changed as America changed. Store modernization and improvement, curtailed during war by shortages and restraints, began it all. Big stores became bigger, became more streamlined. Time- and effort-saving devices were installed. Air conditioning became commonplace. Improved lighting, more modern equipment, the latest conveniences were introduced into the courtship of the postwar consumer. This overview, in simplest terms, sketches what followed during the 1946–1971 period.

The large so-called discount stores, relatively unknown with few exceptions before World War II, made their presence really felt in the early 1950's and really prospered thereafter.

As postwar emigration from cities accelerated its pace, as more and more people crowded into the suburbs, and as more suburbs developed to meet the onrush, consumers were pursued into suburbia not only by newly created branches of department stores but also by chain stores of all kinds.

Once neighborhoods' corner grocers, grocery chains now brought larger and larger supermarkets to big-city neighborhoods, to Main Street locations and to suburban shopping meccas. Individually owned supermarkets, local at start, spread to other locales and became multi-unit enterprises. Department stores became "horizontal" as well as "vertical" as their branch stores swelled in number. Variety store and general merchandise chains became "vertical" as well as "horizontal" as their units expanded in size, in merchandise lines, even in departmentalization. Drugstores continued their diversification away from their former pharmacy identity and became, in effect, variety stores to even greater degree.

Shopping centers consisting of complexes of retail establishments dotted the trade areas of municipalities coast to coast, and gained incredible popularity.

As time passed, sharply rising costs of operation necessitated even sharper cost control. As a constructive yet cost-conserving shopping accommodation, self-service was consequently adopted by more and more volume retailers and was accepted as a convenience by more and more consumers.

So as to broaden base and to attain greater profitable sales volume vitally needed to cope with sharply rising operating costs, many retail organizations diversified. Some bought other chains, in their own or other fields. Some merged. Holding companies bought control of well-established retail corporations and made them components of their compounds of business acquisitions. Some parent chain-store corporations became both holding and operating companies—in effect, conglomerates controlling manufacturing and other types of businesses while centrally owning and managing, or ultimately controlling, two or more distinct chain-store companies, here and abroad.

Woolworth Flexibility Meets Era's Challenge

In the midst of this growing retail-field upheaval, so rife with increasing diversification, mergers, acquisitions, and deeper penetration into fertile retail fields as population swelled, F. W. Woolworth Co. reached and celebrated its 85th Anniversary in 1964.

Led first by its sixth President, James T. Leftwich, who had succeeded Alfred Cornwell in 1955, then by Robert C. Kirkwood, seventh President, who ascended to Woolworth leadership in 1958, the company wrote a brilliant record of achievement in the decade between its Diamond Anniversary in 1954 and its 85th year of life in 1964.

Under these leaders, Woolworth expanded its operations in the variety-store field during that span. Furthermore, again demonstrating its resilience and its readiness to adjust to changing times, it made several bold, rewarding departures from its wholly variety-store heritage, without, of course, altering its prime status as a variety-store chain.

For the first time in its long history, Woolworth penetrated another retail field. It entered the discount-store field by creating a chain named Woolco Department Stores. Under that aegis, it opened its first Woolco store in Columbus, Ohio, in June 1962. Averaging 110,000 square feet of "all-on-one-floor" sales space and 1,000-car parking lots, Woolcos were intended to accommodate, conveniently, consumers seeking demand staple and promotional merchandise, including many brand names, at competitive prices. Consumers liked these stores, made them successful. By midsummer 1964, some 13 such Woolcos dotted the United States and Canada.

In August 1963, Woolworth took another giant step to broaden its base and expand its volume by diversification. Under Kirkwood, it entered the shoe business by acquiring and assimilating the G. R. Kinney Corporation, a well-known shoe-manufacturing and shoestore chain born in 1894.

American Woolworth's traditional indifference to print advertising also altered during that 1954–1964 period, largely influenced by the changing promotional needs of highly competitive retailing.

Frank Woolworth, as seen, had drilled his sights on "impulse buying" by consumers. He wanted his stores to be where heavy traffic existed, and he wanted as much as possible of that human flow to enter his stores. "Let the customer see and handle the merchandise," he constantly counseled. Make "red-fronts" a fairyland of inspectable merchandise, and consumers would walk a mile to browse them, was his deep-rooted judgment. And consumers did. And in doing so they supported his conviction that Woolworth "red-fronts" needed no national print advertising to draw throngs to their wide-open display of "plums" and "corkers" for "impulse buying" purpose.

As the Woolworth network developed, there was occasional local advertising to promote a store anniversary or to herald a store opening. There was also occasional cooperative advertising sponsored by sources of supply. There was a brief experience with network radio. And for several years dating from New Year's Day, 1952, Woolworth sponsored the televising of the Tournament of Roses parade in Pasadena, California, over the complete NBC–TV chain.

But there never had been any national print advertising before 1954. Woolworth use of magazine and newspaper advertising accelerated thereafter. It reached the retail advertising big league a decade later. For 1964, under President Kirkwood, it contracted for some 40 million print lines of advertising nationally so as to stimulate sales for upgraded and expanded merchandise values saturating Woolworth stores.

Without any diminution whatever of its variety-store character and leadership, moreover, Woolworth entered the restaurant field per se with Harvest House cafeterias and restaurants. These, of course, were supplementary to the in-house restaurants, luncheonettes, soda fountains and other such departments located within its "red-fronts" from as far back as the turn of the century.

Additionally, Woolworth rapidly established itself in the new, larger regional shopping centers of the country. To such centers, it brought large, modern stores loaded with upgraded and expanded values.

As Robert Kirkwood stepped up to the Board Chairmanship on January 1, 1965, and was succeeded as President by Lester A. Burcham, Woolworth's eighth in 85 years, he and his predecessor, James Leftwich, could look back upon the following additional achievements attained during that standout decade sandwiched between Woolworth's Diamond Anniversary in 1954 and its 85th Anniversary in 1964.

Woolworth variety stores were brought for the first time to

Alaska, Hawaii, Mexico and Puerto Rico. British Woolworth entered Africa and the British West Indies, besides expanding in England, Scotland, Wales and Ireland. Woolworth also grew in Canada and in Germany.

It added 960 new restaurant, cafeteria and luncheonette units in its variety stores. And it also opened 16 Harvest House restaurants and cafeterias.

The company established a new central accounting office, and it also inaugurated an electronic data-process basic-stock-reorder system that would have been sheer manna from heaven to Frank Woolworth, Carson Peck and the others in the Stewart Building days of Woolworth.

It set into motion an intensive personnel-training operation and developed its college-recruitment program.

For the first time in Woolworth history, its District Offices were made Regional Offices. Five were relocated. All were vested with greater autonomy and responsibility. The head of each was elected to the new office of Regional Vice President in the United States, Managing Director in Canada.

It opened 939 new stores, remodeled or enlarged 348 existing stores, relocated 199. And as against 91 self-service units in 1953, the company operated over 1,930 self-service stores in 1964.

During that span, it opened the largest variety store in the world in Denver, Colorado. And in that 1954–1964 period under Leftwich, then Kirkwood, Woolworth sales soared from over $700 million to over $1.3 billion.

$2.8 Billion Sales and Climbing

Four mercantile superstars were posthumously voted into America's first Merchandising Hall of Fame in 1953.

From a slate of over 200 strong candidates submitted by the

heads of 50 major retail corporations, that illustrious four-some had been the overwhelming choice of the nation's financial editors and the distinguished professors of business and commerce who comprised the national jury of selection.

Each of the four had been the founder of a retail institution that had stimulated the effective teaming of mass distribution with mass production to serve the public interest.

Alphabetically, the four merchant princes whose selection was announced at a sumptuous dinner held in Boston, June 30, 1953, were:

The late Marshall Field, founder of Marshall Field & Co. of Chicago, Illinois.

The late George Huntington Hartford, who, with George F. Gilman, had founded The Great Atlantic & Pacific Tea Company, oldest existing chain-store organization, and who had developed it to world's largest in his day.

The late John Wanamaker, founder of John Wanamaker of Philadelphia and New York.

The late Frank Winfield Woolworth, founder of the Five-and-Ten, and father of F. W. Woolworth Co., a household name internationally.

Conceived by the late Joseph P. Kennedy, Boston banker, former American Ambassador to the Court of St. James's, and father of a later American President and two U.S. Senators, the Merchandising Hall of Fame was hailed by President Eisenhower as giving due recognition at last to pathfinders of "our dynamic distribution system without which America's marvelous productivity could not for long be maintained."

About the Chief, his citation read: "To Frank W. Woolworth, Founder and President of F. W. Woolworth Co., who so materially influenced mass distribution, and who created a new theory of merchandising importantly improving American living standards." Half a century after his death, the Woolworth company that had been created by his vision, leadership and enterprise was still taking giant steps forward to that purpose.

Frank Woolworth wrote a challenge to himself and to his successors in 1907: "We have never taken a step backward, and I trust we never will." And in conceptualizing and implementing his master plan in the way back foundation days of the Woolworth syndicate, he had shaped and cemented policies and procedures that, effective in that era, were also flexible enough to meet the blinding pace of changing times ahead while retaining the basic strengths of Woolworth organization.

Each of his successors—Parson, Miller, Deyo, Cornwell, Leftwich, Kirkwood—had, through 1964, aggressively adapted Woolworth to the conditions prevailing during his own administration. Each with his own distinctive brilliance had led Woolworth a notch higher in stature, in volume, and in performance in behalf of the consumer, than when he had assumed command. Hence, each in his turn had met and surpassed the Woolworth challenge of no backward step.

Woolworth resilience, as seen, had already enabled it to enter effectively into the thriving discount-store field; to diversify into the shoe and restaurant fields; to burgeon in shopping centers; to adjust well to self-service; to adapt profitably to so many other demands of changed and changing times.

Robert Kirkwood, Board Chairman and Chief Executive Officer, and Lester Burcham, President, led American Woolworth from 1965 through its Ninetieth Anniversary in 1969. Chief Executive Officer Burcham, now also Board and Executive Committee Chairman, and John S. Roberts, ninth President, were at American Woolworth's helm as the 1970's brought their vast economic and social challenge.

During the 1965–1971 period, the accelerated pace by which Woolworth broadened its spheres of operation by expansion into other fields while concurrently reinforcing its variety store might, here and overseas, attained record proportions.

It added Kinney Shoes of Canada to its fold in 1965. Then, in March 1969, in the forepart of its 90th Anniversary, it penetrated the men's clothing manufacturing and retailing field by acquiring Richman Brothers Company, an apparel chain store corporation of long standing. Through its Kinney Shoe Corporation later that same year, it also acquired Williams Shoe Ltd. operating 61 shoestores in Australia. And before year-end, both H. Lewis & Sons and the Fred Lewis Corporation became Kinney acquisitions, bringing with them 50 shoestores and two warehouses located in Montreal and the Maritime Provinces.

Despite these effective broadenings of operating base, American Woolworth's fundamental character, focus and identification, however, remained primely concentrated in the field that it had pioneered and in which its name was a household word internationally.

A doubling of population and the vicissitudes of five decades had metamorphosed that field since Frank Woolworth's death. Five-and-Tens, including bellwether Woolworth, that had evolved to variety stores in the pre–World War II period were later graduated to general merchandise store status. The transition is illustrated, simply, by the identity change of their own national trade association. Originated as the Limited Price Variety Stores Association in 1933, it became just Variety Stores Association in the 1950's, then Association of General Merchandise Chains in the late 1960's.

American Woolworth, that once was, and still is, the epitome of "horizontal" retail distribution, became also a full-fledged "vertical" retailer—just as most major department stores became "horizontal" as well as traditionally "vertical" mercantile establishments.

Big Woolworth stores became bigger. They abounded with variety. Related lines of merchandise were both broadened and deepened. In the general merchandise pattern, they met their publics with even more sharply defined and grouped departments. Departments literally became "shops within stores."

The company's gigantic, "new look," so-called "dominant" stores actually were clusters of multifarious shops under one roof—bringing full-line, upgraded values to consumers, priced as close to cost as Woolworth's vast buying power could peg them, with fair profit. According to one Executive Office buying superintendent, "Today's 'dominant' stores are fueled by a new high-octane, big-ticket merchandise mix, but Woolworth's 'sparkplugs' are still its variety lines."

Back in the 1890's, long before Woolworth's "new-breed" emporiums of the 1970's, the Chief coached his store managers to create a sales environment so pleasant to consumers that they would regard browsing and shopping Woolworth as, in effect, going to a fair. He stressed that "fair" bit again and again and again. Emphasis in 1971 was not far off. "Thanks for shopping Woolworth—it's the fun place to shop." And the lovely young lady who said so on the company's television commercial messages seemed and sounded as though she spoke for the company—and that Woolworth said what it meant and meant what it said.

"Remember that our advertisements are in our windows and on our counters," Frank Woolworth wrote to store managers in a General Letter in the company's yesteryear. Both media are still invaluable, but Woolworth supplemented them in 1971 with spot television commercials reaching well over 60 million viewers in some 40 top markets, together with well over 100 million lines of newspaper advertising. From scratch, as seen, in the 1950's, Woolworth in 1971 ranked among the nation's largest retail users of newspaper advertising.

As 1971 ended, therefore, American Woolworth was basically the same in identity, structure and policy, but broader in range of business involvement. Its unbroken momentum was still forward-headed as more and more new and old customers sought its values at its prices. As it had done in each passing era, it was acquiring a "new look." In keeping with the times, its outlook was "upbeat and on the move."

Parent company of American Woolworth was, of course, F. W. Woolworth Co., the successor of F. W. Woolworth & Co. and the merged businesses of Knox, Kirby, Charlton, C. S. Woolworth and Moore; the successor of Frank Woolworth's individually owned syndicate that had been mothered by the tiny Lancaster store from which Frank Woolworth had started it all.

F. W. Woolworth Co., aside from its own vast general merchandise and prepared food service operations[8] in the United States and Puerto Rico and its fast-growing Woolworth Department Stores, was the operating and holding company, as 1971 closed, with 100 percent voting power, of these diverse possessions:

F. W. Woolworth Co., Limited, Canada, including Woolworth Realty Co. plus Findlay's Pharmacy, Ltd.

F. W. Woolworth Co., G.m.b.H., Germany, including F. W. Woolworth G.m.b.H., Austria.

F. W. Woolworth Co., S.A. de C.V., Mexico and Woolworth Española, S.A. (Spain).

The Richman Brothers Company, an Ohio corporation.

---

[8] American Woolworth is now the world's largest in-store food handler. It serves about a million diners daily.

The Kinney Shoe Corporation, New York, including Kinney Shoes of Canada, Ltd.; Norvell Tie Co.; H. Lewis & Sons Co.; Fred Lewis Shoe Corporation, and William Shoe, Ltd. (Australia).

In addition, American Woolworth controlled, by 52 percent ownership of voting power, F. W. Woolworth and Co., Limited, Great Britain—the infant that had been sired by Frank Woolworth in 1909, and which had been built to substantial stature from scratch by his three American and one English "Volunteer-Pioneers." At year's close 1971, that 62-year-old, British-oriented mercantile goliath operated 1,108 British Woolworths and five British Woolcos (the first in Leicester in 1967), in England, British West Indies, Ireland, Scotland, Wales and Africa.

F. W. Woolworth Co., that began life as such in 1912 with 596 Five-and-Tens in the United States and Canada (besides controlling British Woolworth), owned or controlled up-to-date Woolworth general merchandise stores at year-end 1971, thickly dotting not only the U.S.A. mainland but also Alaska, Austria, Africa, British West Indies, Canada, England, Germany, Hawaii, Ireland, Mexico, Puerto Rico, Scotland, Spain, Virgin Islands and Wales. Woolworth range was now practically global.

Considerable progress was being made, furthermore, in the saturation of foreign retail marketplaces. In Canada, for instance, Canadian Woolworth units spread-eagled the Provinces of the country. They existed in depth in Alberta, British Columbia, Manitoba, New Brunswick, Newfoundland, Nova Scotia, Ontario, Prince Edward Island, Quebec and Saskatchewan. Just as British Woolworth, for example, is ingrained British, so too is Canadian Woolworth deeply ingrained Canadian. Where appropriate, and to the extent desirable, its operations, its communications, its promotional media are bilingual.

As 1971 ended, moreover, American Woolworth also meant shoestores, clothing stores, department stores and restaurants.

The total annual sales of American Woolworth that had speeded past the $10 million mark in 1904, past the $100 million mark in 1918, beyond $500 million in 1946, upward of $1 billion in 1960, above $2 billion in 1969, escalated past the $2.8 billion mark in 1971, Woolworth's 92nd year, and the trajectory of its onward drive was still upheaded.

Phoenixlike Woolworth: Circa 1972

President Nixon capsuled the tone and target of his administration in his State of the Nation address as 1972 began. He said in part:

> Let us reject the narrow visions of those who would tell us that we are evil because we are not yet perfect, that we are corrupt because we are not yet pure, that all the sweat and toil and sacrifice that have gone into the building of America were for naught because the building is not yet done. . . . Never has it mattered more that we go forward together.

For the purpose of continuing to go forward, F. W. Woolworth Co., almost concurrently, announced that it would open at least 30 Woolworths and more than 40 additional Woolco Department Stores in the United States and Canada in 1972. In addition, it announced that it will open 107 more Kinney shoe outlets and 44 Richman Brothers clothing stores. Furthermore, its international operations in the United Kingdom, Mexico, Germany and Spain will also be enlarged. Overall, its expansion program will add about 5 million square feet of retail space to its capacity to serve the consumer.

A proved management team is at American Woolworth's

controls as it thrusts forward to this end in 1972, namely Lester Burcham, Board Chairman and Chief Executive Officer, backed up by John Roberts, President.

The Woolworth Building, New York, continues, of course, as seat of the company's Executive Office, command post of international Woolworth.

The high-ceilinged, marble-walled Empire Room of that headquarters still serves as the office of the head of American Woolworth as the Chief had planned, but it is now neither called that nor is it Napoleonic. Its superb marble fireplace is still in place. But its marble 30-foot-square floor is now carpeted wall to wall; its furniture and furnishings are modern, subdued and handsome; its aura is quietly pleasant and efficient.

Mr. Woolworth's Empire-design mahogany desk, two of his Palace of Fontainebleau throne chairs, his treasured Cleopatra clockpiece that had originally been given to Napoleon Bonaparte by the Czar of Russia, and a number of accouterments that had once graced the Chief's Empire Room are now housed in a museumlike room conveniently near the reception area of the 24th floor. Those and other Woolworth memorabilia are there to be seen, and a lot of visitors take the opportunity to view them.

Managing the Woolworth business in behalf of nearly 110,000 common and some 7,000 preferred stockholders, the Board of Directors now consists of 24 members. On that Board are the Chairman, the President, both Executive Vice Presidents, and seven Vice Presidents of American Woolworth, together with the immediate-past Board Chairman, the heads of British and Canadian Woolworths, and the Presidents of the company's subsidiaries, Kinney and Richman. The heads of several prominent manufacturing corporations also have seats on that Board. And the large framed portraits of the Founders that respectively grace the walls of that room of decision, view four of their descendents in action on that Board, namely two Knoxes, a Kirby, and a Peck.[9]

To meet the heading and demands of its planned forward progress, American Woolworth, naturally, has had to make several departures from its pattern of the past. In the Great Beyond, the Chief's first reaction on viewing them was probably a bellowed, "Great Scott!"—his favorite ejaculation—then that famed Woolworth smile of approbation as he recognized them as price for progress in today's changed and changing times. The first such departure affected hallowed Woolworth ground—the "Corner Store" site on the American Corner of the Public Square of Watertown, New York.

William Harvey Moore started his mercantile on-the-job training on that site in 1857, before the Civil War. From that juncture on, that plot of ground, as seen, played a prominent part in the conceptualization and pioneering of the Five-and-Ten. When the "merged businesses" were welded to form today's American Woolworth in 1912, the Founders designated the site as the statutory Principal Office of the new corporation, F. W. Woolworth Co.

So as both to house the company's Principal Office properly and to serve as a memorial to William Moore, Frank Woolworth, as seen, acted immediately upon Moore's death in 1916 to erect a six-story Woolworth Building on that historic ground. Delayed by America's entry into war, the edifice was finally completed and opened in 1921, about two years after the passing of the Chief. For some 45 years thereafter, it served its intended dual purpose.

[9] Besides the Chief's daughters [Footnote 6], descendants of the Founders who have served on the Woolworth Board include Allan P. Kirby (son); Fred M. Kirby II (grandson); Seymour H. Knox (son); Seymour H. Knox III (grandson); Richard W. Woolworth (son of Sum); Fremont C. Peck (son); Carson C. Peck (nephew and a former Vice President); and Andrew F. Peck (grandson).

By 1966, in the new times of that day, it was patently clear to American Woolworth that, except possibly as a shrine, the edifice, to all intents and purposes, had outlived its usefulness. It was terminated that year as the corporation's Principal Office. The Woolworth Building, New York, became the statutory Principal Office as well as the Executive Office of American Woolworth.

As a deeply ingrained part of the Watertown community, Woolworth, in 1969, donated not only that entire building but also all of its leaseholds to the Henry Keep Home of the municipality. "Our action," said President John Roberts, "expresses our belief that this site will thus continue as a useful and 'living' memorial, rather than as a mere relic of the past."

A year later, on June 23, two ceremonies successively occurred in Watertown, of significance not only to that North Country city but also to American Woolworth. At the first, a Woolworth commemorative plaque on the erstwhile Woolworth Building was fittingly unveiled by President Roberts. And at the second, in the very heart of the city's Court-Arsenal Street Urban Renewal Development intended to pump new economic life into Watertown, Woolworth opened its strikingly modern, new and very large Woolworth store.

Occupying some 65,000 square feet of space directly across the Public Square from the "Corner Store" site, the new Woolworth beauty was conceived by Woolworth planners as a "junior department store." "The fact that this Woolworth store opens directly across from where the Woolworth concept was born," said John Roberts, "symbolizes a significant retailing cycle. It represents the progress of a company that has served the American public for over ninety years. And the American Corner site will perpetually remind us of the values associated with experience and tradition in meeting the demands of Woolworth's loyal customers."

The passing of the "Corner Store" site as Woolworth's Principal Office was, at least in part, also cause for another effect. During the 1912–1966 period that it served in that statutory capacity, it was also locale of the corporation's Annual Meeting held yearly at high noon on the third Wednesday of May. That changed in 1966.

Frank Woolworth's Utica "Great 5¢ Store" experience, as seen, taught him the importance of bringing his store to traffic, instead of relying upon traffic to find his store for shopping purpose.

Through his daily General Letters, moreover, he brought information, orientation, motivation, and a sense of involvement and identification to his store managers, instead of wholly relying upon them to come to him for such intelligence, inspiration and sense of belonging. It may parenthetically be added here that, substantially for the same purpose, without, however, resembling its ancestor General Letter, American Woolworth recently launched a 16-page, professionally edited tabloid newspaper titled *Woolworth World,* bringing a potpourri of company and employee news and information to over 70,000 of its personnel at all levels.

And in the very year that Woolworth moved its Principal Office from Watertown to the Cathedral of Commerce, it also started bringing its Annual Meeting to its stockholders, instead of requiring them, year after year, to journey to the North Country of the Empire State for meeting attendance. Breaking away from a 54-year practice so as to square with the needs of these days, it held its Annual Meeting of 1966 in San Francisco and attained wide shareholder attendance, and therefore, more face-to-face exposure of its plans and performance. Ever since, each Annual Meeting has been held, on the usual third Wednesday in May, in a different city. Lancaster, cradle of Woolworth, was the site in 1969, the company's 90th Anniversary.

Not too long before that birthday, it made another bold, timely departure from its past in order to fortify its future.

Some 82 years before that decision, meaning back in 1886,

Frank Woolworth, as seen, opened his tiny first headquarters on Chambers Street in New York. He believed that his thriving little network of Five-and-Tens was now ready to have a device or a service mark that would identify it as a mercantile entity, and his stores as elements of that syndicate. Accordingly, he designed his Diamond W. It made its debut on the front door of that first Woolworth office.

"I remember you felt that first office was quite an undertaking and you took me down to see it," wrote William Moore to him years later. "You said, 'What would you put on that door?' I must have had a vision of present days when I suggested a circle representing the world. The trademark that you decided on was a little more modest but I notice it got there just the same."

The Diamond W's identifying power grew as Woolworth's reach became regional, then national, then international. Through the years, its remembrance power has been incredible. It is probably as well known by the public as Victor's "His Master's Voice"; as the face of Gillette; as the bearded Smith Brothers; as the roaring lion of MGM; as the English-script-lettered nameplate of *The New York Times;* as Fisk Tire Company's long gone but not forgotten "Time to Retire"—and as other identifying devices of long-time proved effectiveness. Along with The Great Atlantic & Pacific Tea Company's "A & P," the Diamond W is perhaps unique in the retail field in terms of longevity and broad performance.

In the earliest day of Woolworth, in the era before the proliferation of chain stores had accustomed the public to recognize stores that were operated under central management, ownership or ultimate capital control, the Chief acted to give his units a uniform store-front appearance. He decided upon red as basic color. He agonized over shade. Finally he chose carmine. Teaming his "red-fronts" with the Diamond W, he made the buying public visibly aware of the Five-and-

Ten generally and of Woolworth specifically. Woolworths became "Everybody's Stores."

Change begets change, and American Woolworth that, as precepted by its sire, has capitalized on every change in the last nine-plus decades, has overhauled its merchandising concept, as seen, so as to dominate the demands of today's new times and to broaden its horizons for tomorrow. In the general merchandise field, its emphasis is on huge, "new look," full-line "dominant" stores, particularly in high-traffic points.

In the implementation of that "new look," a look that "will tell consumers, at a glance, that Woolworth is upbeat and on the move," American Woolworth decided, in 1968, to drop the Diamond W in favor of an, in effect, Rectangle W, a distinctively designed W, centered upon a rectangle-shaped field—and to phase out its famed carmine-red store signs with gold lettering in favor of "brush stroke" blue nameplates.

About that step, then Chairman Kirkwood wrote:

> Next year's 35 new Woolworth stores will be projecting this new image from the outside-in with a "brush stroke" blue nameplate that is the chain's new up-to-date corporate symbol—a new-look logo that will be phased into every level of the company's farflung domestic and international operations in the years ahead.
>
> It will appear in all newspaper advertising here at home next year; on more and more Woolworth home-brand packaging in the years ahead, and on older stores all over the nation as they're remodelled and updated to fit the chain's new "dominant" store mold.
>
> This bold step in corporate image is designed to represent the new-look at Woolworth from the outside-in. But the real impact of the new-look is coming from the inside-out. . . .

Though changed times and Woolworth's flexible adjustment and adaptation to them have resulted in a broader operating perimeter and the façade, in effect, of a mercantile conglomerate, the chain of basic policies forged in the company's yesterday has fundamentally endured unbroken to this day.

Consumer acceptance, championed, developed and practiced by Woolworth's syndicate from birth, is as much Woolworth policy now as ever.

Offering consumers of every age and kind, everywhere, a fairly standard stock of modern basic goods, sweetened by an ever broadening and deepening variety of expanded and upgraded novelties, fads, fashion goods and other attractive values, all priced as close as possible to cost, is still a bedrock principle governing the "vertical" store operations of this 93-year-old "horizontal" mass distributor.

To accomplish such result, quantity buying, direct from source, for cash, nourished by quick turnover and large-volume sales, are more-than-ever predicates of Woolworth procurement. Its "buy-sell" relationship with a very long, diverse list of producers dates practically from or near the turn of the century. Most of them grew as Woolworth grew.

American Woolworth's own production facilities and warehouses exist in the United States, Canada, Mexico, Puerto Rico and Spain. Its modern warehouses are, of course, a far cry from Frank Woolworth's far smaller first free-standing warehouse, successor of his Reshipping Department, located first in his Newark store, then transferred to the 14th Street, New York, "red-front." Opened in 1910 on Hudson and Vandam Streets, New York, that first warehouse was rented by Woolworth, "from the Rector, Warden and Vestrymen of the Trinity Church."

Interaction of Woolworth-oriented experts of various kinds at interfacing store, region and headquarters levels, each spurred by the incentive of profit-sharing pioneered by Frank Woolworth in 1884, still generates the company's forward thrust. Its reservoir of leaders, in various stages of their development, is still piped from bottom up. Its input is speeding as its accelerated training program is quickening the readiness of Learners to move up the Woolworth ladder.

The circle of Woolworth's central buyers, visualized in the Chief's 1888 master plan and started with Carson Peck's ascent to the New York Office in 1890, is still composed of professionals of unassailable qualifications, competitively achieved during long-time, store-up Woolworth association. They ferret out the values, for store order, that consumer demand in stores has itself dictated. They introduce new "buys," at Woolworth prices, for consumer consideration through store tests. As production experts, just as Woolworth buyers have been doing since the Chief started it all, they assist producers of real values to meet Woolworth standards of quality, quantity and price, with fair profit to themselves and Woolworth.

In the past of the company, store managers, as seen, were supervised, inspected, assisted and served by District Offices, the first of which, F. W. Woolworth & Co.'s old Chicago Office, was opened in 1904. When the present American Woolworth corporation was formed in 1912, with eight District Offices in the U.S.A. and Canada, it was probably the first chain-store company not only to achieve coast-to-coast stature but also to decentralize its administrative functions.

To keep ahead of today's faster-paced times, and abreast of its own "on-the-move" momentum, American Woolworth, instead of District Offices, now has seven Regional Offices in the United States. Each is calculatedly well-supplied with expertise, manpower, equipment and other requisites, to operate effectively, in the modern manner, a moderate-size, high-volume regional chain store enterprise that is headed forward. Each led by a Regional Vice President who, in effect, is the head of a regional chain store company, these Regional Offices are the catalysts, shepherds, liaison channels, clearing-houses, service agencies, and all else, to the respective stores,

ranging 200–325 each, that are under their respective juris-
dictions.

Woolworth stores continue to court heavy traffic, and continue to be located where heavy traffic exists, be it a big-city
site, a Main Street locale, or a shopping center in suburbia.
And they are big stores, getting bigger. By the standards of
that day, for example, the Chief's first store in Boston, opened
in 1896, was a big "red-front." By comparison, American
Woolworth's newest store in that city, opened in 1970 in a
downtown multimillion-dollar urban-development area, has
133,410 square feet of building space and four sales floors.
That spectacular new unit has a location traffic flow of
250,000 people a day. It is the biggest Woolworth store in the
world in terms of lineal feet of counters. It abounds in in-store
specialty shops.

That Boston example is an illustration of Woolworth's mass-
volume approach in action. It demonstrates continued ad-
herence to the Chief's precept of making shopping convenient
and pleasant for customers while providing them with wide
choice of quality merchandise at the lowest possible price.

Skyqueen at Sixty

Some six decades, four American wars, and a more than
doubling of the nation's population after the Woolworth
Building's 1913 dedication, Frank Woolworth's skyqueen and
F. W. Woolworth Co. itself are, as stated, hale, current and
competitive. Built to last, both have surmounted the vicissitudes of those 60 eventful years.

Under the stimulus of fresh leadership drawn from its own
brimming reservoir of company-groomed merchants—H. T.
Parson after the Chief, then B. D. Miller, C. W. Deyo, A. L.
Cornwell, J. T. Leftwich, R. C. Kirkwood, and now, L. A.
Burcham—the company, like the legendary phoenix, has, in

stride, refreshed and reoriented itself to fast-changing times, but has never taken a step backward. And the Woolworth Building has kept apace.

The so-called Cathedral of Commerce, once hailed as "Queen of the New York Skyline," and now probably "Queen Mother," is no longer the world's tallest office building by a wide margin. But a lot of admirers, adult and even some young, native and even some alien, insist that it would still be a formidable contender in any beauty contest of skyscrapers. And some of its lovers would back the loveliness of its external lines and tracery against all comers still.

Now the twelfth tallest building in the world, and ninth highest in the Empire City, it has grown older gracefully. Without losing its famed charm, it has kept step with modern times through multimillion-dollar modernization programs.

Costing Frank Woolworth a then astronomic $13.5 million in cold cash to erect a structure of the Skyqueen's stature and class on that historic Lower City plot, experts consider it impossible even to estimate how much it would cost to build today, or how long it would take to erect it. One reason is that its superb lace-in-stone exterior ornamentation and its exquisite interior marblework were painstakingly produced by master craftsmen, now deceased or superannuated, whose skills are rarely practiced, or rarely even to be found, today.

Aside from housing the Executive Office of F. W. Woolworth Co., its Northeastern Regional Office, and the headquarters of its Kinney Shoe Corporation, the Cathedral of Commerce today has some 250 other tenants, including a number who have been occupants since its 1913 opening. The Irving Trust Company, which in 1913 had its Main Office in the building, is still a tenant though its Executive Office is now elsewhere. Famous past tenants include the now historic, though then "hush-hush," Manhattan Project. Always fully rented, its long waiting list of yesterday is as long today.

It still offers convenience, besides comfort and elegance.

Two subway lines have stations in its basement, and a third is only a block away.

Renovation projects have included complete central air conditioning, with individual room temperature control; 24 even higher-speed elevators; even brighter lighting throughout the edifice; an up-to-date power plant; and a steam substation.

The Skyqueen's famed Observation Tower that used to draw a quarter of a million viewers yearly, remained popular until 1941, when the Navy ordered it closed because it afforded too good a view of ships in the harbor. It was never reopened, to the disappointment of so many couples who had visited it while on Manhattan honeymoon and who wanted to relive the experience.

When it reigned as Skyline Queen, the Woolworth Building was the unofficial welcomer of seafarers as they put into New York Harbor. In the halcyon day of passenger travel on the great transatlantic liners of that era—R.M.S. *Mauretania,* S.S. *Leviathan,* S.S. *Aquitania,* S.S. *France,* S.S. *Berengaria,* the lot—incoming passengers would line the decks to look first leftward for the Statue of Liberty, then rightward for the Skyline Queen.

Today's fewer inbound transatlantic voyagers still look leftward and quickly find Miss Liberty. Rightward, it is no longer easy to spot the Queen Mother in today's crowded skyline court.

Still-Posted Sentinels

High upstairs in the Woolworth Building, the command post of American Woolworth, under Chairman Burcham and President Roberts, conducts the international affairs of the business so modestly begun by a young farm-bred man with a vivid mercantile vision in a wee Lancaster, Pennsylvania, emporium openly displaying and selling Yankee Notions at fixed nickel-and-dime prices, in the "shin plaster" days of 1879.

Downstairs, in a niche high on the marble wall of the Grand Arcade, a statuette of the great building's sire and father of the upstairs international enterprise, fixed there some sixty years ago, still silently observes as traffic passes by.

And both the company and the building, by their up-to-date capacity to perform their function, serve to keep green the memory of the young Lancaster merchant who, the New York *Sun* said, "won a fortune not in showing how little could be sold for much, but how much could be sold for little."

By their continued progress, they give even greater meaning to the resolution adopted by their sire's peers on the Board of Directors of F. W. Woolworth Co., shortly after his passing in 1919:

. . . This Board, bowing with humility and reverence to the Great Architect of the universe, records with grief too deep for words, the passing away of the founder of this business.

His business foresight, his keen judgment of men, and his kindly helpfulness to even the lowliest of his employees, which enabled him to establish this business are examples for us all to emulate.

We have lost a great light—his counsel and wise judgment will be sadly missed. His kindly smile and winning personality which were so instrumental in the growth and development of this business, will ever be a cherished memory.

The "Cathedral of Commerce" whose lofty spire reaches to the heavens and marks his fame as a merchant prince, is but a small monument compared with the love he inspired in the hearts of the men associated with him in business, from the highest to the lowest. Their love being infinite, it is therefore the greatest monument of all.

Index